Our
Heavenly
Home

Also by E.X. Heatherley

The
Parables
of
Christ

Our Heavenly Home

E. X. Heatherley

BALCONY PUBLISHING

Austin, TX 78734

Abbreviations
for Versions of the Bible

¤ ASV   *The American Standard Version*
¤ AV   *The Authorized (King James) Version*
¤ RSV   *The Revised Standard Version*

Note that quotations not otherwise credited are from the Authorized (King James) Version.

Published by Balcony Publishing, Inc., Austin, Texas

Library of Congress
Catalog Card Number (Applied For)
ISBN 0-929488-97-0

10 9 8 7 6 5 4 3 2 1

Printed in the United States of America

Dedicated

to

Dr. George C. Boone

Son in the faith
Friend 'til death
Brother in the Lord...forever

From the Publisher

Our Heavenly Home originally was penned, edited, and published by E. X. Heatherley some forty-five years ago. This, the fourth edition, is being published posthumously and is the first printing of this work to be produced for and distributed through regular trade publishing channels. We at Balcony Publishing were particularly determined to engage editorial and cover design talent who could meet turn-of-the-century literary and design standards while remaining faithful to the heart, meaning, and style of the author.

The book you are now reading speaks for the editors, **Mike** and **Jennifer Plake**, and the cover artist and designer, **Dennis Hill**, in actual demonstration of their skills and dedication to excellence. If the editors have been successful (and we believe they have), reading this edition will be done with greater ease and comprehension, but with little noticeable difference between this and the latest rendition from the author.

Our warmest thanks to Mike, Jennifer, and Dennis.

—*Balcony Publishing*

Table of Contents

From the Author

It would be impossible to acknowledge all my debts to those who have contributed in various ways to this testimony—the devoted Mother who first encouraged me to study the Word of God, the noble Pastor whose teaching brought me to a knowledge of the Truth, the faithful Helpmeet who has shared unfailingly in all my labors, and the many fellow saints who have been my partners in the propagation of the Gospel down through the years.

May the hope of heaven cheer your heart and brighten all your days!

—*E. X. Heatherley*

Our Heavenly Home

In thy presence is fullness of joy. At thy right hand there are pleasures for evermore!

King David

Precious Prospects

Long before the New Testament was given to complete the revelation of God's gracious plans for us, the prophet Isaiah, perceiving that the future held in store far better things than the ancient saints had ever experienced under the Law, made this significant allusion to the dawn of a brighter day:

> *...Eye hath not seen, nor ear heard,*
> *neither have entered into the heart of man,*
> *the things which God hath prepared*
> *for them that love him.*[1]

This, of course, has already had its initial fulfillment in the personal experience of those of us who have received the Gospel, and, as Paul declares, we are even now endowed with "all spiritual blessings in heavenly places in Christ."[2] However, it is obvious that Isaiah and Paul peered far beyond the horizons of the present world and contemplated the prospect of a fuller realization of this blessedness in the heavenly sphere. According to both, as well as all the other sacred writers, we may be confident that for all of us who are sincerely trusting the Lord Jesus Christ, "the best is yet to be!"[3]

The Best is Yet to Be!

Thank God for this beautiful earth and all the rich provisions He has made to ensure our welfare and happiness here and now. Even so, according to His promises, we may rejoice in the assurance that He is reserving something incomparably better for us, as the chosen heirs of His sovereign love.

Heaven! What a delightful thought! How dear the hope! More precious, day by day! What cheer the prospect brings to these faint hearts of ours, as increasing cares and the mounting weight of passing years combine to overwhelm our spirits with frustration and disillusionment!

Sooner or later we, like Abraham in the days of old, discover that we have here on earth "no continuing city." We find ourselves wishfully looking for "one to come." Each day intensifies the feeling that we are "strangers and pilgrims on the earth." More and more, we cherish the prospect of a "better country" beyond this present "vale of wrath and tears."

This longing itself is doubtless a divinely-given down payment on the blessing it anticipates, inspiring us to nourish ourselves on these expectations while we wait for our inheritance. The youthful build their hopes upon the mists of dawn. The healthy launch their optimistic conquests under the fleeting smile of a noonday sun. Those who succeed enjoy the fickle favors of fortune for a while. But after youth has flown, health is gone, and earthly aspirations recede before the advancing shadows of senility and death, then, turning from the wreckage of our shattered dreams, we scan the farther banks of Jordan and long for home.

Nor is this experience peculiar to the aged and dying. It is the common lot of Christian people wherever stress or disaster exposes the transitory nature of our earthly pilgrimage.

When quite a young man, I spent several months in the hills of western Kentucky—I think, by providential arrangement—distributing Bibles among humble mining folk. They needed the Bibles; I still lacked some lessons I had not received in school. While working in that rugged area, I attended many simple Gospel services in which poor laborers, ridden by the rigors of the Great Depression, poured out their souls in fervent testimony, song, and prayer. Despite their hardships of poverty, sickness, and discouragement, they seemed to share the uplifting inspiration of a common hope. I was especially impressed with their ardent singing—homely, perhaps, but buoyant with a note of joyous expectancy.

One of their favorite songs, I recall, ran something like this:

This world is not my home,
   I'm just passing through;
If heaven were not my home,
   Lord, I don't know what I'd do!
Loved ones beckon me
   To heaven's open door,
And I cannot feel at home
   In this world any more!

That was their triumphant answer, on one hand, to unemployment and, on the other, to long hours, hard work, and low pay. It was their confident retort to the ever-present specter of privation, disease, and death. Nor were they merely "whistling in the dark;" they meant what they sang. In fact, I have rarely witnessed such transparent sincerity. Like ancient Israel in the "waste and howling wilderness," they were living on the corn of Canaan, sight unseen. Having experienced the merest foretaste of the wine of Eschol, they esteemed no hardship too grievous to bear if it seemed to shorten the distance to the cluster-laden vineyards of the Promised Land!

It may be that you have never heard that quaint old song; the "better churches" have "better music" nowadays. But do we not voice the same exultant sentiment in many of our more "respectable hymns"? Take, for example, those familiar lines:

> *One sweetly solemn thought*
> *Comes to me o'er and o'er;*
> *I'm nearer my home today*
> *Than I have been before!*

How pleasantly the zephyrs of Canaan brush our cheeks as we join in this refrain! And, likewise, when we sing:

> *There's a land that is fairer than day,*
> *And by faith we can see it afar;*
> *For the Father waits over the way,*
> *To prepare us a dwelling place there!*

The songs of the saints may vary as to form and literary quality; but, in any case, the yearning they express is quite the same.

Glimpses of Glory

When, as a boy, I used to hear the old folks sing, "I would not live alway!" I was rather perplexed at their seemingly pessimistic attitude. But with the passage of years, as I too grow older, it is gradually becoming easier to appreciate their point of view.

Brother John Ward

Old Brother John Ward, a day or two before he crossed the swollen Jordan, told me why a way-worn pilgrim wants to travel on.

There he lay among the gathering shadows, with a bandaged stub where a gangrenous foot had been. His worn-out body throbbed with mortal pain, and the solemn hush of death already was in his voice. Still, he clasped my hand affectionately.

In a rather confidential way, he exclaimed, "Brother Heatherley, my destined hour has come. I am about to lay this body down. But that's all right. Our sovereign Lord knows best. He planned the end from the beginning. I want to say to you that the end is good. I'm going to that 'city that has foundations, whose Builder and Maker is God'!"

A few days later, nature yielded to the summons of heaven. That stalwart old Gospel preacher completed his wilderness journey and settled down to rest in "the land of pure delight."

Sister Mary Hodges

Dear old Sister Mary Hodges, likewise, took

me into her confidence when she stood on Mount Pisgah's brow.

"Brother Heatherley," she whispered, "yesterday morning the Lord came here to my bedside. He led me away to see the beautiful city, took me through the streets of glory, and showed me my mansion over there. After that, He brought me back to bid the rest of you farewell. I just can't describe to you what I saw! It was too wonderful for any words I know—too wonderful, I'm afraid, for some folks to believe. I'm not telling this to everybody, Preacher; just to you. Some people might think that I am only feverish and out of my head, and they might not believe me. But you believe me, don't you?"

I assured her that I did believe in the reality of her experience. And I still do. No doubt, in some mysterious manner beyond our present comprehension, she, like so many other saints when they gazed through the twilight to "the land of cloudless day," beheld the glorified Saviour and our heavenly home.

On the following night, at her own request, I held her frail, emaciated hand while she reached forth with the other, healthy as Gabriel's, to greet her waiting friends on the other side. Once again, I found it was becoming easier to understand what the old folks meant when they used to sing, "I would not live alway!"

Brother Lewis

I learned still more from my final visit with Brother Lewis, out in the sun behind his house one bright Monday morning a few years ago. An invalid who had suffered patiently for many years, he was sitting alone on an old cane-bottomed chair. It was a touching sight, especially to one who knew him so well—such a manly person in such a helpless condition! There he sat, with his crutches on the ground beside him. He was ailing, hurting, waiting.

"Brother Lewis," I said, "I want to read you a passage from the Book of Isaiah; I think it will cheer your heart to hear what God is going to do for His afflicted people at a future day."

He listened intently. Tears streamed down his face when we came to those lines that say:

Then the eyes of the blind shall be opened,
and the ears of the deaf shall be unstopped.
Then shall the lame man leap as an hart
(a wild deer), and the tongue of the dumb
sing . . .[4]

I felt, as I closed the Book, that this millennial passage has a timeless message—a glimpse of glory to encourage the hearts of languishing saints in every land and age.

"Mr. Lewis," I went on, "I know it must be hard for you to sit here helpless and suffering as you watch so many other people coming and going at will. But, according to this and many other Scriptures, it will not be long until you will be able to 'leap as an hart' and walk the streets of glory with the rest of us."

We prayed together, as we often did, and then I bade my dear old friend farewell. I think he knew, as I myself somehow suspected, that his trials were almost over. However, I doubt that even he was aware how soon deliverance would come. Word came to me in scarcely more than twenty-four hours that he had been taken home. He had laid aside his crutches, once for all, and, like another "lame man" of a former day, begun a new and happier career at the Beautiful Gate.

During the funeral service, it seemed to me that I could hear his footsteps resounding in the heavenly temple court. As I once again read those lines, "Then shall the lame man leap as an hart," I felt that he was still listening, but smiling now instead of weeping. Finally, as we lowered all that was left of his afflicted humanity into the grave, a sense of sweet relief swept over my spirit. To my surprise, I found my own heart sighing, "I would not live alway!"

"Better and Better!"

Brother J. A. Stigall

How precious this conviction becomes as, in the course of time, we see "the saints go marching in!" No one who knew him after his remarkable conversion will ever forget Brother J. A. Stigall and his radiant smile. He first heard the Gospel and found himself trusting the Lord Jesus Christ one dark, rainy night at a little cottage service out in the country about two miles from town. He was 72 when the Good Shepherd finally "drew" him into the fold. When the summons came he meekly "followed on" and was, quite literally, "charmed to confess the voice divine."

I had just tried to preach on the latter part of the 16th chapter of Acts, concluding, as I usually did, with my favorite invitation:

*...Believe on the Lord Jesus Christ,
and thou shalt be saved...*[5]

As we sang *Just As I Am*, I prayed with all my heart—and seemed to pray in vain. But during the closing stanza, after my faltering faith had well-nigh failed, God "reached down His hand" to rescue His wandering sheep.

There was a sudden commotion over in the corner at the left of the big stone fireplace where Brother Stigall was trying to make his way through the startled crowd. He came tottering across the rough-hewn floor to where I stood. Half-blinded with tears, he paid no attention to my outstretched hand but, instead, threw his arms about me and wept for joy. And from that night on, he was one of the happiest Christians I have ever known.

Hundreds of those who used to attend our extension services back then remember the heavenly light that always shone from his face as he stood, from time to time, and gave his testimony. Excitedly, he praised the Lord for "that Easter Saturday night" when Jesus saved him "in that little service out on King's Mill Road."

"Go back?" he would say, "Why, there's nothing to go back to! I have just what I want, and there's nothing better than this!"

But he eventually learned that there is something even better than the "milk and honey" that so completely satisfy a newborn babe in Christ. A few years later, on one of his visits in my home, he joined us in our noonday meal. I called on him to ask the blessing. I can only say that "Heaven came down our souls to greet, and glory crowned the mercy seat!" He prayed, and wept between his words, addressing the Lord as if He were sitting there with us at the table.

I have heard all kinds of prayers—by deacons, preachers, college professors, and various other people. But I have yet to hear a sweeter or more inspiring one than Brother Stigall's as he poured out his heart that day. Once more, he gave his testimony—this time, directly to God, as if oblivious of the presence of anyone else—rehearsing his experience. Step by step, he was thanking the Lord, again and again, for "that Easter Saturday night" when he "was changed from nature to grace." When he had finished, tears were coursing down the furrows of his face. The luster of glory sparkled from his eyes.

Reaching impulsively across the corner of the table with both hands, he took me by the wrists and, almost shouting, asked, "Brother Heatherley, will it keep on getting better and better?" Delighted to see him learning that one's conversion marks only the beginning of an endless march of triumph, I was thrilled at my own renewed appreciation of that precious truth.

"Yes, Brother Stigall," I answered. "Yes, it surely will. It will keep on getting better and better as the days go by. As wonderful as it is to taste the first-fruits of eternal joy, we are just 'beginning to make merry' now!"[6]

A short while afterward it became my duty to preach beside his casket. Recalling the recent experience in my dining room, I felt that nothing could be more comforting to his loved ones than to tell them of his own discovery.

"My friends," I said at the conclusion of my message, "you have often heard Brother Stigall relate the story of his conversion and describe the blessedness that came into his heart one 'Easter Saturday night'."

"That was indeed an inspiring testimony, and it will be greatly missed in our meetings. But if we could hear him now, I am sure he would say: 'Don't grieve for me; I'm happy, and there are no regrets. Go back? Not me! There's nothing to go back to; I have what I want, and it keeps on getting better and better'."

Thank God for death, for sweet release from every earthly ill, for heaven's open door, and for prevenient grace that makes it possible for weary souls, sustained by lively hope, to sing, "I would not live alway!"

Each time we bid some cherished friend farewell, the hope of heaven deepens in our hearts. Every time we dig another grave, that hope grows brighter.

Oh, the loved ones who are waiting for us over there! And how they multiply from year to year! In losing, we gain, until eventually, our heavenly interests outweigh all earthly treasures. Like Paul, we find ourselves "in a strait betwixt two, having a desire to depart, and to be with Christ."[7] The saints of the ages are there—the patriarchs and prophets of old, the holy apostles, the faithful martyrs, and all those whom we have "loved long since, and lost a while." Best of all, our blessed Lord is there! Oh, for the day when we shall see His face and, as a "great multitude, which no man can number," lift our voices together in the glad redemption song!

Does not your heart, my dear reader, "burn within you" at the prospect of that day? I am sure, and sincerely glad, that it does. For not the least of heaven's blessings will be this, that all of us shall be together and in perfect accord. Forever free from loneliness, we shall revel in the blessed thrill of sweet togetherness. Certainly, we will be with Jesus, surrounded by "old familiar faces," in the Father's house, where "there are pleasures for evermore"![8]

But it may be that your vision of glory is marred by misgivings about some aspects of our future state. Because this is generally true, we shall now proceed to examine a few of the principal questions that seem to bother most of us at one time or another.

If in your case it is otherwise, then you are all the better prepared to enjoy a review of the familiar truths we are about to discuss. It is undoubtedly the will of God that we should rejoice together in our hope of glory. Since it is impossible for anyone to face the future hopefully, without disquieting doubts, unless he knows what the Scriptures have to say about the other side of death, we must inform our faith by appealing to the Bible as the final source of competent evidence.

Not that we shall, even there, find all the answers; for where the Scriptures are silent, we must be content to "walk by faith, not by sight."[9] But, there is ample information in what has been revealed to satisfy our hearts, if not our minds, about the rest.

First, then, let us consider the question which necessarily precedes all others: *Does heaven really exist?*

---

[1] I Corinthians 2:9. [2] Ephesians 1:3.
[3] Apologies to Browning.
[4] Isaiah 35:5, 6. [5] Acts 16:31. [6] Cf. Luke 15:24.
[7] Phillipians 1:23. [8] Psalms 16:11. [9] II Corinthians 5:7.

In my Father's house are many
mansions: if it were not so,
I would have told you.

Jesus Christ

Does Heaven Really Exist?

In the absence of tangible evidence, how can we—prone by nature to question anything that is not sensory—make sure an unseen realm actually exists? No astronomer has ever sighted heaven's towering spires with a telescope. No chemist has scrutinized its foundations with a microscope. No mathematician has produced an equation that requires its existence as a logical necessity. And no philosopher has been able to undergird his wishful premises with substantial proof.

The Dictates of Reason

Nevertheless, sheer reason finds sufficient

grounds in what we know intuitively, to postulate the existence of another, better, world.

What we know about the nature of God requires us to expect some such provision for His children. The visible creation testifies not only that He exists, but also that He is infinitely wise, all-powerful, and inherently good. Can we believe that such wisdom is thwarted by the enigma of death? Should we think that such power is halted at the border of the grave? Or that such goodness lures us with hope, that it may mock us with despair? Pure reason needs no other proof than that exhibited by nature to warrant the rejection of such palpable absurdities.

What we know about the nature of man compels us to look forward to something better, in a better world. The marvelous constitution of the human personality implies an immensely higher and nobler destiny than anyone can realize in three-score years and ten. Man is a wonderful creature, the connecting link between two worlds—one spiritual and invisible, the other natural and tangible—for, unlike all other earthly creatures, he belongs to both. His body is natural. His soul[1] is spiritual. Death separates the soul from the body. But the soul—that is, the human *ego*—is elementary and, therefore, indissoluble and, hence, cannot be destroyed. We all have an intuitive consciousness of this remarkable fact. Sooner or later, all except a few inveterate agnostics admit that our destiny, in its fullest measure, must be realized beyond this present life.

This is altogether reasonable. Consider such endowments of human genius as those of Michaelangelo, Shakespeare, Handel, or Albert Schweitzer. All exhibit far more resources than a single lifetime can develop or exhaust. However mediocre some of us appear to be, this is true of all people. If modern psychologists have done nothing more, they have conclusively demonstrated that every one of us has immeasurably more latent potential than we are normally conscious of. Is it rational, then, to suppose that God has thus endowed us, only to resign such undeveloped powers and properties to the grave? Can we believe that Michaelangelo has spent his genius and forever laid aside his brush? Or that Shakespeare, who wrote so much, so well, will write no more? Or that Charles Haddon Spurgeon will never preach, nor Ira D. Sankey sing again? Why, the greatest of men have scarcely enough time here on this planet to advance beyond the kindergarten stage.

It is unthinkable that the kind of God we have has made us the kind of creatures we are that the flame of our personalities might flicker for a few brief decades and then disappear forever, at the dissolution of our mortal frames! Such an irrational hypothesis both mocks the Maker and ignores the demonstrable excellence of His handiwork.

Again, the universal hope of immortality, felt and cherished by all kinds of people in every land and age, cannot be explained except through the assumption that it comes from God and will eventually be gratified. The universe is so ordered that some special provision may be found for every requirement and some adequate supply for every need.

For instance, there is water for thirst, food for hunger, light for the eyes, and sound for the ears. On this principle, we may be assured that God has made ample provision for the ultimate satisfaction of our inherent hopes. It is inconceivable that a benevolent Maker, being who and what He is, would endow us with an instinctive yearning for a more abundant life, while planning to requite our expectations with eternal nothingness!

The Testimony of the Scriptures

Pure logic demands a larger opportunity, in a more propitious environment, for the people of God. Our spiritual growth simply will not stop at death. However, this felicitous opportunity will be forfeited by incorrigible sinners who persist in willful, suicidal unbelief. Not that our hope is dependent on sheer reason, however; for we, indeed, have a "more sure word of prophecy," an infallible revelation from God, which is infinitely more reliable than even the most convincing arguments from any other source. Such a revelation lifts us above the plane of fallible reason to the higher ground of moral certainty. *For the Bible everywhere assumes, and frequently asserts, the glorious reality of our heavenly home.*

The very first verse in Genesis mentions heaven and provides a pregnant introduction for the more extended treatment it receives in many subsequent passages: "In the beginning God created the *heaven* and the earth." Contrary to the rendering of our popular version, the word here is "heavens"—neither singular nor plural, but dual. It indicates the *two* "heavens," the natural and the spiritual, produced by the original creative act. However, after Jesus' resurrection, when "paradise" was moved from Sheol-Hades into God's own celestial abode, three heavens are alluded to in the record—the atmospheric, the stellar, and the paradise-like "third heaven." But this is evidently a phenomenal usage, accommodating language to the human point of view. In no way does it present a real contradiction to the Genesis account.

The Old Testament abounds with allusions to heaven as the site of God's eternal throne and the dwelling place of a myriad of holy angels. However, as we shall see a little later, it was not accessible to the souls of justified people until after the resurrection of Christ.

The Scriptures, even the earliest of them, are replete with intimations of a future life:

◻ Job gazed beyond the dismal ashes of temporal disaster and shouted: *...I know that my redeemer liveth, and that he shall stand at the latter day upon the earth: And though after my skin worms destroy this body, yet in my flesh shall I see God: Whom I shall see for myself, and mine eyes shall behold, and not another; though my reins be consumed within me.*[2]

◻ David was equally confident when he exulted: *Thou, which hast shewed me great and sore troubles, shalt quicken me again, and shalt bring me up again from the depths of the earth.*[3] And again, *As for me, I will behold thy face in righteousness: I shall be satisfied, when I awake, with thy likeness.*[4]

◻ And Isaiah, addressing his discouraged nation, declared: *Thy dead men shall live, together with my dead body shall they arise. Awake and sing, ye that dwell in dust: for thy dew is as the dew of herbs, and the earth shall cast out the dead.*[5]

Indeed, a number of the ancient prophets were granted special visions of the glory world:

◻ Micaiah saw the heavenly court in formal session before the throne of God.[6]

◻ Ezekiel looked beyond the firmament and saw

the Son of God presiding as the Lord of Providence.[7]

⌷ Daniel saw Him sitting in judgment amidst the awful splendor of eternal majesty.[8]

The New Testament, as we might expect, devotes still more attention to heavenly things and adds much luminous information to the body of evidence from the Old Testament:

⌷ The birth of our Lord was announced by an angel from *heaven* and celebrated by a celestial choir.

⌷ The Saviour, during His teaching ministry, constantly spoke of *heaven* as a glorious reality. He claimed to have come from *heaven*; proposed to establish the kingdom of *heaven*; and repeatedly alluded to the Father in *heaven*, the angels of *heaven*, and the disciples' reward in *heaven*.

No one who is familiar with His preaching can believe in Him without acknowledging the existence of our heavenly home.

Time and again, down through the ages, heaven's mysterious precincts have been seen, its voices heard, and its nearness felt, by specially-privileged saints:

¤ Elisha saw Elijah wafted skyward on the wheels of a fiery whirlwind. Shortly afterward, Elisha's servant beheld the armies of heaven in full array.

¤ At the time of our Lord's transfiguration, Peter, James and John were allowed a glimpse into the unseen realm where Moses and Elijah conferred with Jesus within the aura of the glory-cloud.

¤ Later on, the eleven apostles saw the risen Saviour ascend to heaven from the crest of Mount Olive.

¤ Still later, Stephen saw the heavens opened and Jesus standing at God's right hand.

¤ The apostle Paul was caught up into paradise, or "the third heaven," where he received unutterable revelations from the Lord.

¤ John the Revelator witnessed the marvelous celestial panorama he describes in the Apocalypse.

And that's not all. Countless other saints have gazed beyond the twilight in their dying hours, and left their testimony that they saw the "lights of home"!

Even more often, voices from heaven have greeted believing ears. The Father's voice was heard:

- ♮ at Sinai in the wilderness.

- ♮ at the Saviour's baptismal scene.

- ♮ at the transfiguration.

- ♮ and again, in the court of the temple during Passion Week.

Since then our glorified Lord has, on a number of known occasions, conversed from heaven with his followers on earth—with Saul on the Damascus Road and at least two other such occurrences; with Peter at Joppa; with John on the Isle of Patmos; and, perhaps, with many others, maybe you.

Sometimes we feel a consciousness of heaven. Our hearts "burn within us" when the presence and power of God are manifested in some special way. Have you not sensed the sweet aroma of that pleasant land, while standing on the brink of Jordan with some departing friend? Have you felt the joy of heaven in your heart when some lost sheep was brought into the fold, or when some wayward prodigal returned? Oh, yes, our hearts are in conscious rapport with those who exult in the choir lofts of glory, even now!

What need have we, with such assurances as these, for further proofs dependent on human sight? We have the promise of the Father, the Son, and the Holy Spirit. We have the declarations of the patriarchs, the prophets, the apostles, and the holy martyrs. And we have the testimonies of departing loved ones who have viewed the good land from Jordan's nether shore. Meanwhile, there is a mysterious voice within us that speaks for both intuition and faith, to certify the unimpeachable reliability of our hope. You may be assured, my friend, that heaven is a glorious reality; and in all probability it is better, bigger, and nearer than you think!

But it may be that your heart keeps asking, *Where is heaven?*

---

[1] For the moment, to avoid confusing the mind of the ordinary reader, I am using the word "soul" in its popular sense, as being synonymous with "spirit." Strictly speaking, the soul is only *immaterial*, not necessarily *spiritual* – the invisible counterpart of the visible body. But since the human soul is vitalized by a God-given spirit, it, unlike the soul of a lower animal, is usually thought of as being identical with the human spirit itself.

[2]Job 19:25-27. [3] Ps. 71:20 [4] Ps. 17:15. [5] Isa. 26:19.
[6] Cf. I Kings 22:19. [7] Cf. Ezek. 1:26. [8] Cf. Dan. 7:9, 10.

Where Is Heaven?

This question assumes that heaven is a *place*, and rightly so. Such is not only the consistent teaching of the Scriptures, but also a logical necessity. A single conclusive statement from our Lord's own lips is decisive for everyone who believes His Word:

"I go," He said, "to prepare a place for you . . . that where I am, there ye may be also."[1]

Three things stand out in this significant utterance:

¤ First, Jesus expressly refers to heaven as "a place."

¤ He reveals that He will be there.

¤ He declares that we, too, shall presently join

Him there.

These propositions must stand or fall together. Heaven has to be a *place* in order to accommodate the glorified body of the risen Lord, as well as our own when we receive them later on. The existence of a body necessitates the existence of a place for that body to occupy. It is simply impossible for any real object to exist outside some area in space. Therefore, a thing that is "nowhere" is no "thing" at all, but *nothing*—nonexistent. Those, then, who insist that heaven is only a "state" are actually—though, doubtless, unintentionally—contending that death annihilates the personality. They are claiming that Jesus, not to mention the rest of us, has no real existence as a corporate personal entity beyond the grave.

Such fallacious teaching is essentially the same as the pagan Hindu doctrine of "Nirvana," which holds forth the gloomy prospect of personal nonexistence after death. Or should this be denied, there is the subtle rejoinder that the individual, by merging into "the universal Brahma," merely loses his identity as an individual. In the final analysis the difference is only rhetorical, not real.

This theory solves no problem at all.

Even a "state" is inconceivable apart from its concomitant locality. Even a disembodied spirit, so far from being ubiquitous, must occupy some definite point in space at any given time.

Even if, as the Hindus teach, it somehow coalesced with a vague, omnipresent "universal soul," that all-pervading "soul" itself would have to subsist in *universal* space. There is no less a "place" because of its vast extent.

So, we must conclude that every personality is either local, universal, or extinct. Therefore, any "heaven" occupied by resurrected bodies is bound to be an actual locality, not merely some kind of theoretical state existing within an indefinable void.

It is easier by far to simply believe God's Word, than to reconcile human theories to known realties. The Bible consistently teaches that our heavenly home, however spiritual in its nature, is as truly substantial as the grosser matter of the visible world, though incalculably more refined.

The Geography of Glory

It does not follow, however, as many people suppose, that heaven is a relatively small domain remotely situated "far beyond the blue." How easy it is for us to veer from one extreme to another or to misconstrue a fragment of truth for the whole!

Our heavenly home is neither some sort of nebulous "state" without a setting, nor merely an isolated region in the sky. It is a spiritually-conditioned cosmos having no frontiers and no forbidden bounds, save only that it excludes the abysmal prison of the damned.

In comparison with heaven, hell is like a tiny cavern submerged in a shoreless sea—an isolated penal dungeon lost in the bottomless depths of a boundless universe. In the Scriptures it is always alluded to as being "down"—which, from every human point of view, the world around, positions that dreadful place of punishment in the heart of the earth.

Modern scientists usually estimate that the outer crust of our planet is approximately thirteen miles thick. They generally agree that underneath this peripheral surface of water, rock, and clay, there is a veritable caldron of molten stone convulsing with indescribable heat. What a "lake of fire and brimstone," and how close it lies beneath the sinner's feet! It is amply large for the incarceration of Satan, the wicked angels, and impenitent people who spurn the overtures of grace—eight thousand miles from brim to fiery brim—but, otherwise, of no appreciable significance in a setting measured only by infinity.

Heaven, on the other hand, is always mentioned as being "up":

¤ From the dawn of time the saints have lifted their faces skyward when in worship and prayer.

¤ The risen Lord was "taken up"[2] into heaven.

⌑ Stephen, in the hour of his death, "looked up"[3] to the resplendent scene where Jesus stood at the right hand of God.

⌑ Paul was "caught up"[4] into the glory world, when he received his remarkable fore-glimpse of "the land that is fairer than day."

Wherever men are situated on the geographical earth, at any point of the compass in any hemisphere, they find themselves beneath the vaulted ceiling of the Father's house. In keeping with this universal fact, it is apparent that heaven surrounds our planet like cosmic space. We are, all of us, encircled by its nearness and vastness alike.

The heavenly Canaan is, then, quite literally, "a good land and large"! It provides "a large place,"[5] as the psalmist says, for our expanding fortunes in the ages to come. There is abundant "room" for the boundless dominions of our sovereign Lord—for myriad angels, countless saints of ages past, all elect believers yet unborn, and the multitudes who will be raptured when Christ returns! There will be room for every one of us to have a mansion nestled in his own exclusive celestial estate—abundant room for eternal conquest, development, and growth! Oh yes, our Father's house is "good" and "large"—as splendid and spacious as infinite wisdom could devise for infinite power to build!

Think of it! Astronomers tell us that the moon is about 240,000 miles away in distant space, the sun some 93,000,000 miles still farther, and the stars unnumbered billions of light-years from our little earth.

There is room, I tell you, in our Father's house!

We are told that 500,000 planets such as ours could be compressed within the circumference of the sun and that uncounted galaxies of immeasurably larger "suns" are being sighted almost every passing year. All this, they see through their increasingly powerful telescopes. Still, they have yet to peer, with their strongest lens and largest mirror, beyond the immediate threshold of our heavenly home!

Strangely enough, however, there are more than a few misguided literalists who propose to compute the dimensions of the "better country." One of them claims to have ascertained that heaven is considerably smaller than America. He estimates there will be only room enough there for every heir of grace to occupy a cubical apartment 16 by 16 feet in area!

Such consummate nonsense is due, at least in part, to a general but needless misunderstanding of John's description of the New Jerusalem, this despite the fact that John at no time refers to the "holy city" as "heaven." He tells us, instead, that the New Jerusalem is "the bride, the Lamb's wife." This language clearly presents a symbolical depiction of the glorified Church. Instead of being identical with heaven, it will descend "*out of heaven from God.*"[6] It is not called "heaven," but is said to be *from* heaven. It is heavenly, in heaven, and of heaven. But it stands in relation to heaven as, shall we say, a capital city is related to the empire of which it is a part. As to the specified dimensions of the city itself, the record makes it clear that they are figurative, being used to "signify"[7] spiritual truths.

I repeat, the Scriptures assign no boundaries to heaven itself, so vast are the expansive dominions of our heavenly home!

Just Beyond the Veil

Another popular misconception stands in need of correction here. Most people seem to think that heaven is a long way off—"beyond the starry sky," to use a common phrase. And it is true that the far-flung battlements of glory do embrace the nether reaches of boundless space. Moses mentions "the heaven of heavens."[8] Paul declares that Jesus "ascended up far above all heavens."[9] But while such passages suggest ineffable remoteness, there are many others in which the nearness of the better world is asserted with equal clarity. Heaven is at once both near and far—much nearer, and farther, no doubt, than most of us have ever dreamed.

If this seems paradoxical, a simple illustration may be helpful. The ocean can be no nearer to anyone than to a person, any person, swimming in it at any given point. Yet, to such a swimmer most of its enormous mass is a long way off. Likewise, heaven is as near to us as water to the skin. It is also as distant as the ultra-mundane breakers of a universal sea!

Our Lord, in this connection, made a remarkably revealing statement in His famous interview with Nicodemus. Standing visibly in His fleshly body, right before the Jewish ruler's eyes, He casually observed that "...no man hath ascended up to heaven, but he that came down from heaven, even the Son of man which is in heaven."[10] Though clothed with our flesh and living as Man among men, the Saviour was conscious of being "in heaven" all the while!

This, of course, was true of Him in a particular sense. I do not suggest that we can realize a consciousness of heaven's nearness to the same extent. But the fact itself, however dimly we perceive it, is incontestable.

We are in the midst of heaven all the time. The only barrier between us and our loved ones in glory is a veil of flesh. When that veil is rent in the moment of death, the beatific vision will appear. It will be instant, without any interim of waiting. There will be no "journey," or at least there need be none. When our bodily "tent" collapses we shall find ourselves "at home" right where we are. We will be in the Father's house. We shall be surrounded by the holy angels and face to face with our departed friends and loved ones who have been hovering all around us every day.

We are already on the invisible scene of our inheritance, and the intervening veil hangs only on another heartbeat and another breath.

If some Elisha should prevail with God to unshutter our eyes, as when the servant-lad's were opened to behold the chariots over Dothan,[11] we, too, would see the hosts of heaven all about us. We would discover that, however lonely, we are never alone. This, I believe, is precisely what the apostle pictures in Hebrews 12:1, where he declares that "we also are compassed about" with a "great cloud of witnesses." Like the contestants in an ancient Roman stadium, we are running life's race before the eyes of many solicitous witnesses who, having finished their course, are waiting to share the laurels with the rest of us![12]

This brings us, naturally, to another question of tremendous moment: *When do we go to heaven?*

---

[1] John 14:2, 3. [2] Acts 1:9. [3] Acts 7:55. [4] II Cor. 12:2.
[5] Ps. 18:19. [6] Rev. 21:10. [7] Cf. Rev. 1:1. [8] Deut. 10:14.
[9] Eph. 4:10. [10] John 3:13. [11] Cf. II Kings 6:17.
[12] Cf. Heb. 11:40.

And they heard a great voice from heaven saying unto them, Come up hither.

John the Apostle

When Do We Go To Heaven?

There are those who contend that no one has ever yet gone to heaven. They claim that when Christians die, they lapse into a state of absolute unconsciousness, and that the souls of the deceased must "sleep" until the resurrection morn.

There are others who teach that disembodied believers retain their personal consciousness but pass through an intermediate "purgatory," where they are cleansed by fire preparatory to entering heaven at a later time.

It matters very little who may advocate, or object to, such theories on rational grounds. Only the Word of God is competent to speak with certainty concerning the future and the state of the dead. "What saith the Scripture?" is, therefore, the decisive question. It is only by appealing to divine revelation that we may inform ourselves reliably about such things.

According to the Scriptures, it is true that, prior to Jesus' resurrection, those who died in the faith were not transferred immediately to heaven but, instead, were kept in detention until after they had been redeemed at Calvary.

In the 16th chapter of Luke, our Lord reveals the lot of those who died in former times. He described the cases of a certain rich man and a beggar who lay at his gate. The rich man died and his body was buried, but he himself descended into the abode of departed spirits, which was known as "Sheol" by the Jews and as "Hades" by the Greeks. Then Lazarus, the beggar, also died and he, too, was committed to Sheol-Hades. But, whereas the rich man languished in a flame of fire, the beggar was comforted.

This represents the normal experience of the wicked and the righteous, respectively, before the death and resurrection of Christ. In both cases, their bodies returned to the dust and their spirits were confined in Sheol-Hades. But the wicked were kept in a place of torment and the righteous in "Abraham's bosom," with an impassable "gulf" between the place of comfort and that of woe.

There was nothing arbitrary or accidental about this arrangement. It was necessitated by moral conditions that only the cross could remove on behalf of believers and that made judgment mandatory in the case of the impenitent. The righteous dead of the old dispensation had based their hope upon the promise of the coming Saviour's redemptive ministry. In the purpose of God, of course, they had been redeemed from all eternity, in the same sense that Christ is "the Lamb slain from the foundation of the world."[1] But they could not be ushered into heaven until the great redemptive transaction had actually taken place. As believers, justified prospectively, they were kept from the punitive flame. However, they had to remain in detention in "the lowest parts of the earth"[2] until the Saviour came to ransom and deliver them.

Zechariah, contemplating the condition of the saints in Sheol, called them "prisoners of hope."[3] As God's prophetic mouthpiece, he foretold their release and transfer to a more felicitous abode. Foreseeing their liberation in connection with the coming Messiah's triumph over death, he wrote:

> *Rejoice greatly, O daughter of Zion: shout, O daughter of Jerusalem: behold thy King cometh unto thee: he is just, and having salvation; lowly, and riding upon an ass, and upon a colt the foal of an ass.*[4]

Then Zechariah foretold the degradation of unbelieving Jewry and the extension of the Gospel to the Gentile world:

> *And I will cut off the chariot from Ephraim, and the horse from Jerusalem, and the battle bow shall be cut off: and he shall speak peace unto the heathen: and his dominion shall be from sea even to sea, and from the river even to the ends of the earth.*[5]

At this point, and against this background, God the Father is represented as assuring the risen Saviour:

> *As for thee also, by the blood of thy covenant I have sent forth thy prisoners out of the pit wherein is no water.*[6]

And then, addressing the anxious "prisoners" themselves, the Father is quoted as saying:

> *Turn you to the strong hold* [that is, to the heavenly Zion], *ye prisoners of hope: even to day do I declare that I will render double unto thee.*[7]

These "prisoners of hope" were, in fact, the original members of the Church, the Body of Christ. Together, they composed what might be called the holy "fetus" which was destined to experience its corporate "birth" when Christ, its Head, arose as "the First Begotten of the dead."

Our Lord Himself had prophesied by David's pen to the same effect:

> *I will praise thee* [the Father]; *for I am fearfully and wonderfully made: marvellous are thy works; and that my soul knoweth right well.*[8]

This refers to the formation of Christ's Mystical Body *(the church)* by the decree of the Father, during its embryonic development in Sheol-Hades. It is the only interpretation allowable in the light of the ensuing verse, in which Christ goes on to say:

> *My substance* [Hebrew for "body"] *was not hid from thee, when I was made in secret, and curiously wrought in the lowest parts of the earth.*[9]

The formation of the church "in the lowest parts of the earth" was an unrevealed "mystery" during the old dispensation—a secret "hid in God;"[10] but instead of being hid *from* God, it was a preliminary factor in His master plan—the creation, redemption, and glorification of a "bride" for Christ!

And so, our Lord, therefore, continues:

Thine eyes did see my substance [body],
*yet being unperfect; and in thy book all
my members were written, which in con-
tinuance were fashioned, when as yet there
was none of them.* [11]

This plainly means that the Church is composed
of God's elect, who were "chosen" in Christ "before the foundation of the world." [12] Not only did
He have their names recorded in the book of life,
but also "what days they should be fashioned". [13]
In short, He determined the time of their incor-
poration in the Church, both in respect to their
individual experience and their relation to the dis-
pensational calendar.

Our Lord, in His famous declaration to
Simon Peter at Caesarea-Philippi, undoubtedly
alluded to the impending liberation of the nascent
Church:

*And I say also unto thee, That thou art
Peter* [petros, a stone], *and upon this rock*
[petra, a massive underlying ledge: here,
figuratively, Christ Himself as just confessed by Peter] *I will build my church;
and the gates of hell* [Greek, Hades] *shall
not prevail against it.* [14]

The customary interpretation of this utterance is

52

misleading and unwarranted by both the language of the local text and the general drift of the larger context. It is usually explained as meaning that the powers of Hades can never destroy the visible historical Church. This is a proposition which is elsewhere flatly contradicted in a number of eschatological passages,[15] but which is altogether alien to the subject under consideration here. Nor can the figure Jesus used be thus construed with any show of reason; it would be utterly illogical to represent "gates" as being aggressive instruments of destruction. As stationary fixtures, they are naturally of a defensive, never an offensive, character. It is of their nature and purpose to restrain or forbid, to keep somebody either in or out, not to attack or destroy. Therefore, when the Saviour declared that the gates of Hades should not "prevail against" the Church, He obviously meant that Hades would soon be impotent to any longer restrain its "prisoners of hope."

For millenniums the gates of Sheol-Hades had prevailed in keeping the embryonic Church within its prison-womb.

But, after our Lord's redemptive death and His triumphant resurrection, they could no longer enforce the confinement of the Church for whose deliverance He died.

Though still a hidden "secret" to the world at large, the Church was constantly before the mind of Jesus as a precious reality. He knew that shortly after the vicarious travail of the cross, His mystical body would breathe the breath of life as an organic entity. This epochal occurrence would come about by virtue of the all-important truth which Peter had just confessed—that Christ's redemptive ministry as the incarnate Son of God would lay the moral ground for the realization of the Church's glorious destiny.

At that point in history, this involved the liberation of the imprisoned saints from Sheol-Hades. So now, with only about nine months remaining until that great event, which was to be accomplished in connection with His resurrection, He spoke of it as an imminent certainty.

It may be worthwhile to note what Peter himself, to whom these words were originally addressed, had to say in subsequent Scriptures in regard to their significance. He was in an ideal position to evaluate their meaning and to testify concerning their fulfillment when the time arrived.

In his initial sermon, on the Day of Pentecost, he cited Psalm 16:10 to show that Jesus, after His death, was not left in Hades—which certainly implies that the Saviour went to Hades when He died.[16] In his First Epistle he tells us why:

> *For Christ also hath once suffered for sins, the just for the unjust, that he might bring us to God, being put to death in the flesh, but quickened* (in) *the Spirit:* [that is, His

54

own personal human spirit] *By which*
[His own personal spirit] *also he went
and preached unto the spirits in prison...*[17]

This language, as far as it goes, reflects our Lord's
reply to Peter's "great confession" and corrobo-
rates our own interpretation of the Saviour's remarks on that occasion. He was put to death in
the flesh. His body was laid in Joseph's rock-hewn
tomb. But His spirit, as He Himself had foretold,
descended into "the heart of the earth" and remained there for three days and nights.[18]

In other words, He went to Sheol-Hades,
which, according to both David and Paul, is in "the
lower parts of the earth." There, He is said to
have "preached unto the spirits in prison." Here
the reference, in keeping with the apostle's local
line of thought, is to the disobedient people who
lived before the Flood.

We are bound to infer, however, from the
writings of Paul, that the disembodied Saviour established contact with the spirits of the righteous
also. It is clear from all sources that, on the third
day, after having prevailed against the "gates of hell
(Hades)" and released "a multitude of captives,"
He arose and escorted the liberated saints into the
heavenly tabernacle, "that the LORD God might
dwell among them."[19]

Paul, in the 4th chapter of Ephesians, fills in
a number of details which are lacking in Peter's

account.

In the first six verses of that chapter, he insists upon the essential unity of the Church, enumerating seven bonds of spiritual affinity common to all believers and exhorting us to hold this truth inviolate, endeavoring to realize it in our conscious experience. But, in the seventh verse he calls attention to the fact that, notwithstanding our basic unity, we as individuals are very differently endowed with spiritual gifts. At this point, the mention of spiritual gifts apparently turns the apostle's thoughts to those events immediately preceding Pentecost when the diversity of "gifts" was first exhibited among the early saints.

"Wherefore he [the Holy Spirit] saith," Paul continues, citing Psalm 68:18, "When he [the risen Lord] ascended up on high, he led captivity captive, and gave gifts unto men."[20]

Here—supplementing the testimony of David, Jesus, and Peter—the inspired apostle tells us that our Lord, when He ascended from Hades, "led [with Him] a multitude of captives [that is, the old dispensation saints]" and that He afterward (at Pentecost) "gave [spiritual] gifts unto men."

This leads the apostle's thoughts still further back, for he continues:

Now that He ascended, what is it but that He also descended first into the lower parts of the earth?

This evidently means that Jesus, before His resurrection, visited "the lowest parts of the earth," where, according to the psalmist, the mystical Body of Christ was being formed:

¤ He visited Sheol-Hades, whose gates, the Saviour promised, would not prevent the liberation of the righteous dead.

¤ He went to "the heart of the earth," where He had said He would spend three days and nights after being crucified.

¤ He visited the subterranean "prison," where, according to Peter, the disembodied Saviour carried on a preaching ministry.

All witnesses agree. Together, they present a complete account of our Lord's triumphant conquest of the underworld![21]

Among other reasons, we have dwelt at some length on this line of truth in order to draw a contrast between the lots of pre and post Crucifixion believers after death. The Saviour's promise, "I go to prepare a place for you," was fully accomplished in all its moral aspects, when He died to open up for us "a new and living way" into "the holiest."[22] This "preparation" made it possible for the "prisoners of hope" to flee their "pit" and settle down in the heavenly "stronghold." To us, it provides complete exemption from an interim of waiting, with the additional privilege of immediate access to the family circle in our Father's house!

Since Jesus "led captivity captive," no believer has ever gone to Hades. Paradise is now in glory. The very moment a Christian "falls asleep" here, he wakes up there!

There remains no reason for an interval of detention, now that our redemption is an accomplished fact. A conquering Redeemer has vanquished sin, death, and Hades. A priestly Pioneer has blazed a trail to "Canaan's fair and happy land". Each of us may now take up the dauntless apostle's words and say:

> *I am in a strait betwixt two, having a desire to depart, and to be with Christ; which is far better.*[23]

No old dispensation saint could have anticipated death so cheerfully. Back then, there was only Sheol to look forward to. But *we* can do so with undoubting confidence, knowing that to depart is to be—immediately with Christ—in our heavenly home! This, we may be sure, is "far better" than remaining with our dearest loved ones in a world of disappointment, suffering, and tears. It is certainly better than a long internment in "the lower parts of the earth"!

For a believer, then, in this present age, "to

die is" truly "gain."²⁴ Nor only so; it is *immediate* gain! "We are confident," says the great apostle, "and willing rather to be absent from the body, and to be present [or, literally, *at home*] with the Lord."²⁵

Take care to note the various implications in this significant utterance.

To be "absent" here is to be "present" there—to be "at home." This language refutes the idea of an intermediate "purgatory." Nor is there any need for such a fiery cleansing, for Christ has already "redeem(ed) us from all iniquity."²⁶ We are "clean every whit," owing naught to God except a ceaseless debt of gratitude and love. Nor does this passage countenance the gloomy "soul-sleep" theory; it leaves no room for an indefinite period of slumber for the soul. But we shall have more to say about this in dealing with the frequently asked question: *Will we be conscious in heaven?*

---

¹ Rev. 13:8. ² Ps. 139:15; Eph. 4:9. ³ Zech. 9:12.
⁴ Zech. 9:9. ⁵ Zech. 9:10. ⁶ Zech. 9:11. ⁷ Zech. 9:12.
⁸ Ps. 139:14. ⁹ Ps. 139:15. ¹⁰ Eph. 3:9. ¹¹Ps. 139:16.
¹² Eph. 1:4. ¹³ Ps. 139:16, margin. ¹⁴Matt. 16:18.
¹⁵ E.g., Rev. 17. ¹⁶ Cf. Acts 2:31.
¹⁷ I Pet. 3:18, 19. See Appendix.
¹⁸ Cf. Matt. 12:40. ¹⁹ Ps. 68:18. ²⁰ Cf. Eph. 4:8.
²¹A more extensive discussion of our Lord's post-resurrection ministry in Hades will be found in my earlier volume entitled *"The Eternal Purpose"*; but, for the moment, see the

Appendix in this book.
[22] Heb. 9:8; 10:20. [23] Phil. 1:23. [24] Phil. 1:21.
[25] II Cor. 5:8. [26] Titus 2:14.

Will We Be Conscious In Heaven?

Appearances mock the thought! What could be so conspicuously devoid of consciousness as a corpse? And, as for the missing personality, death seems to annihilate the tenant when it destroys his house.

It all comes about with almost incredible unexpectedness, even though one knows precisely what is taking place. The weary hours, so slow but all too fleeting, exact their inexorable toll. Strength gives place to fever, and fever to chill. Breath follows rattled breath at ever-longer intervals. At last, a final pause extends itself too long. Then, suspense is broken with a gasp, a tremulous convulsion, and another pause that never ends. The doctor shakes his head, and anxious loved ones search in vain for some sign of a presence which is no longer there.

Where is he?

Gone.

Gone where?

He was here a moment ago. *He?* Yes, of course—a normal, rational human being—a living *person*. He lived, he thought, he talked. He felt, and loved, and willed.

Do they tell me that he *was*, but *is* no more?

I do not, I cannot, I will not believe it! What if appearances do belie the daring premises of lingering hope? Let appearances perish, as they do, with mortal flesh. When they are gone, their absence proves nothing more than that the spirit has no further need of them! Some hold that one who so recently exhibited such Godlike faculties has suddenly become extinct, to think and love and will no more, existing only in the memories of lingering friends. Such cynical nihilism requires more perverted "faith" than hope needs proof of the soul's survival in another world.

As truly as our physical senses perceive and confirm the actuality of physical death, our hearts are reassured with an inherent awareness that the soul lives on. Enlightened believers have the additional advantage of an unerring revelation. Divinely-instructed faith, instead of looking for the living among the dead, rejoices in the soul's emancipation from the cumbersome inhibitions of a sin-deranged environment.

> *For which cause we faint not; but though our outward man perish, yet the inward man is renewed day by day. For our light affliction, which is but for a moment, worketh for us a far more exceeding and eternal weight of glory; While we look not at the things which are seen, but at the things which are not seen: for the things which are seen are temporal; but the things which are not seen are eternal.* [1]

Jnfallible Proofs

According to the Scriptures, though Abraham died some eighteen hundred years before Christ, and his body still lies in unbroken sleep where it was laid to rest in the Cave of Machpelah, he himself remains alive. For Jesus, who cannot be charged with error, declared that the "God of Abraham" is "not a God of the dead, but of the living."[2]

Likewise, Moses died, and Elijah was caught up alive into the sky. Yet, according to the sacred record, both of them were living, conscious, and articulate when, long centuries afterward, the disciples saw them with the transfigured Saviour on the holy mount.[3]

When Paul was stoned at Lystra, his assailants thought him dead.[4] According to his own account of that event, he possibly was.[5] Yet, during the attendant period of suspended animation, he was conscious of being in heaven, where he heard "unspeakable words, which it is not lawful for a man to utter."[6] He was physically inert, impassive, insensible, and yet in full possession of his personal faculties!

Thus does the Revelator represent the disembodied souls of those who will be martyred during the Great Tribulation—conscious, vocal, robed, and resting in hope.[7]

This state of affairs is obviously not peculiar to any one dispensation. According to the Scriptures generally, it is normal for the personalities of both the righteous and the wicked to persist, and to retain their cognitive faculties, after death.

The case of Dives and Lazarus, though belonging to a former age, reveals that all the dead have always survived the dissolution of their bodies and remained alert to their surroundings in the other world. In Hades, the rich man could see, feel, thirst, remember, and pray; the beggar was capable of receiving comfort; Abraham exhibited unquestionable indications of his former competence. And, besides, both Abraham and Dives were familiar with the then-existing situation on the earthly scene.

In view of this and other passages of like significance, I am personally convinced that our loved ones are not only self-conscious but also conversant with the affairs of the present world:

⌷ When Samuel was called up from the spirit-world by the witch at Endor, to talk with Saul, he spoke of current events as if he had been witnessing the local scene.[8]

⌷ When Moses and Elijah conferred with Jesus on the mount of transfiguration, they were keenly aware of the course of events on earth and discussed the issues involved in the sacrifice the Saviour was about to make.[9]

⌷ The souls of the martyrs John describes as being "under the altar," knew all about conditions in the world and prayed for vindication from the calumny of their earthly foes.[10]

⌷ Our Lord's own assertion that "there is joy in the presence of the angels" when a sinner repents,[11] implies that the saints in glory know what takes place here.

We might go on and on reviewing similar evidences from the Scriptures, but these suffice to illustrate the rest. We are, no doubt, surrounded at this very moment by countless saints of former times who are expectantly waiting for us to join them in our heavenly home!

With such a scene before his mind, the great apostle urges, "Wherefore seeing we also are compassed about with so great a cloud of witnesses, let us lay aside every weight, and the sin which doth so easily beset us, and let us run with patience the race that is set before us."[12]

From what we have learned thus far, it is clear that human souls are fully conscious even in their disembodied state. Therefore, it should hardly need to be said that we shall be in full possession of all our faculties after we have been invested with our new, immortal bodies on the resurrection morn. The evidence supporting this assurance will continue to mount up, however, as we examine what the Scriptures have to say in answer to the following question: *What kind of bodies shall we have in heaven?*

---

[1] II Cor. 4:16-18. [2] Luke 20:38. [3] Cf. Matt. 17:3.
[4] Cf. Acts 14:19. [5] Cf. II Cor. 12:2, 3. [6] II Cor. 12:4.
[7] Cf. Rev. 6:9-11. [8] Cf. I Sam. 28:15-19.
[9] Cf. Luke 9:30, 31. [10] Cf. Rev. 6:9-11.
[11] Luke 15:10. [12] Heb. 12:1.

Our Heavenly Bodies

It is written that, "The LORD God formed man of the dust of the ground, and breathed into his nostrils the breath of life; and man became a living soul."[1] This revealing statement is basic to an understanding of the constitution of the human personality. It is the inspired description of our capacity for the realization of the seemingly limitless aspirations of our hearts. It certainly indicates a combination of physical and spiritual properties in a single personal entity. Therefore, it implies that the soul must occupy a body in order for a human being to be complete.

It is obvious that without a body, no man can realize his ultimate fulfillment or attain to the lofty degree of happiness and usefulness of which he is otherwise capable.

As to his physical nature, the original man evidently was endowed with natural life, mind, and instincts, or, in short, with all the normal faculties of an animal soul—not truly spiritual, but simply immaterial. It was the supernatural infusion of his Maker's breath, enduing him with a truly spiritual nature, that invested him with Godlike personality, moral freedom, a sense of responsibility, and the capacity for indefinite development.

Most of the older theologians recognize this elementary truth but tend to over-simplify it, ignoring the more definitive disclosures of later revelation. They think of man as simply a *bipartite* being consisting of body and soul. They overlook his special enduement with a uniquely spiritual faculty. They conceive of the soul and spirit as being virtually identical.

Such a conception fails to differentiate between the souls of men and those of beasts, implying that animals, also, have a spiritual nature. But the New Testament definitely teaches that we are *tripartite*—possessing *body*, *soul*, and *spirit*—and that it is only by the introduction of a nobler element that our souls are endowed with genuine spirituality.

That the apostle Paul subscribed to this more discriminating view is evident from the explicit language he employed in one of his recorded prayers:

"And the very God of peace sanctify you wholly; and I pray God your whole spirit and soul and body be preserved blameless unto the coming of our Lord Jesus Christ."[2]

In related passages it is either asserted or implied that:

- the *body* is the sensory instrument with which we become acquainted with our physical and temporal environment.
- the *soul*, or self-conscious ego, is the seat of our emotional nature.
- the *spirit*—which, having come from God, is normally capable of knowing and enjoying fellowship with Him—is the dominant volitional faculty of the redeemed personality (though "dead," in the sense of being inert and impotent, in the case of unregenerate people).

So we, like God who made us in His image, are not merely *bipartite*, but constitutionally *triune*.

In our normal condition, body, soul, and spirit are inseparably combined within the fabric of an integral personality. That is why physical death, when viewed objectively by those who lack spiritual discernment, seems to destroy its victim altogether.

Actually, it annihilates neither body, soul, nor spirit, but accomplishes its havoc by dissolving the cohesive relationship between the physical and the immaterial. It is an unnatural divider of that which God has joined together. It *separates*, as when, in that supreme example of its woeful intrusion into the moral order—Christ on the cross—it provoked that terrible wail, "My God, my God, why hast thou foresaken me?"[3] That, not merely the dissolution of the personality, is its ultimate stroke—the separation of its victim's soul from God.

But Christ, by "taste(ing) death for every man,"[4] has made the justified believer invulnerable to its "sting."[5]

Those who are trusting Him will, therefore, never know the terror of the "second death."[6] As for the first death, we are assured that He who "raised up the Lord Jesus shall raise up us also by Jesus."[7]

In other words, the Spirit of God will reverse death's dreadful process, reunite our elemental parts, and reconstitute us in new bodies that can never die!

Our reinvestiture in such immortal bodies is as certain as the fact that Christ, our great Forerunner, has already carried our glorified humanity into the heavens! His resurrection enables and guarantees our own! There is a *Man* in glory—not merely a "spirit," but One having "flesh and bones"[8]—and we shall be both *with* and *like* Him, by and by!

Garments of Glory

We shall not, however, receive our new bodies until the resurrection of the righteous at Christ's return. From the hour of death until that glorious event, we shall remain alive and conscious in the presence of the Lord. But, in the absence of our normal bodily complement, we shall not be able to achieve our ultimate fulfillment during that more or less, though not altogether, quiescent interval. We shall enjoy inestimable "gain" and find our new estate "far better" than our former lot on earth. But even then it may still be said that "the best is yet to be"—when, at the resurrection of the righteous, once again entire, we are clothed with immortality in our glorified bodies. Then we will be ideally fitted for the thrilling conquests of an endless future within the ever-receding horizons of eternal opportunity!

Not that we must tarry in the meantime as naked spirits, hampered and embarrassed by a state of utter disembodiment. While we are waiting for better things we shall be attired in robes of glory, perhaps as Adam and Eve were clothed with the unsullied splendor of soulical holiness before the Fall.

For we know that if our earthly house of this tabernacle were dissolved, we have a building of God, an house not made with hands, eternal in the heavens. For in this [present body of flesh and blood] we groan, earnestly desiring to be clothed upon with our house which is from heaven: If so be that being clothed we shall not be found naked.[9]

This promise probably anticipates our final re-embodiment. It certainly assures us that, in the meantime, we shall be enswathed with the glory of the body which is to be.

The Features of the Soul

Contrary to the common but groundless notion that we shall be formless, ethereal spirits until we get our permanent bodies, the Bible teaches that we shall retain our distinctive personal features all the while. This follows from the fact, suggested by experience and implied in numerous Scriptures, that the soul is the immaterial counterpart of the physical constitution, coinciding with it, line for line and feature for feature, at every point.

Any dubious person who is willing to try, can confirm this fact with experimental proof, right here and now. Those who take the trouble to do so, find it undeniable.

A one-legged man will testify that he can still "feel" his amputated foot and "wiggle" his missing toes. Anyone who wishes may, by concentrating his attention on any particular area of his body, sense the presence of his corresponding soulical member in its physical counterpart.

These simple experiments indicate the merging of the soul and body in identical space and show why the soul, when separated from the body, retains the perfect features of the old discarded house of clay. But we have far better proof than this—real proof, dependent not on our deductions from experience but on the irrefutable implications of many positive statements in the Word of God.

Take, for instance, the case of Moses. His body died and was buried some fifteen hundred years before he appeared with Elijah at our Lord's transfiguration. Though his physical remains still mingled with the dust at Nebo, in an unknown grave, he himself—that is, his soul—was seen, and heard, and recognized by Peter, James and John.

Likewise, the prophet Samuel was seen and recognized after his death by the witch at Endor, and, through her abilities as a medium, he was enabled to communicate with Saul.

In each of these instances the soul, made visible by supernatural means, exhibited the features of the absent body from which it had been released by natural death.

There can be no doubt that the early Christians, as well as many of the ancient Jews, believed this truth. We are told that Peter, after having been delivered from prison, came to the house where the disciples were engaged in prayer for his release. A little girl named Rhoda reported to the praying group that Peter was at the door.[10] The disciples, then taking for granted that he had just been executed, supposed that little Rhoda had seen his "angel" (that is, his *spirit* or *soul*) at the door. They evidently believed that Peter, in his disembodied state, would have the same appearance as before. Many a modern saint will testify to having seen familiar faces during mysterious but undeniable moments of other-than-earthly ecstasy!

A Better Hope

But the future greets us with something incomparably better than the mere retention of our personal features and faculties. We shall have all this and more, far more, when we are clothed with new, immortal bodies at our Lord's return.

Paul puts it this way, in his First Epistle to the Thessalonians:

> *But I would not have you to be ignorant, brethren, concerning them which are asleep, that ye sorrow not, even as others which have no hope. For if* [or, just as] *we believe that Jesus died and rose again, even so* [in keeping with the obvious implication of this tenet] *them also which sleep in Jesus will God bring with him. For this we say unto you by the word of*

*the Lord, that we which are alive and re-
main unto the coming of the Lord shall
not prevent [or, go before] them which
are asleep. For the Lord himself shall descend from heaven with a shout, with the
voice of the archangel, and with the trump
of God: and the dead in Christ shall rise
first: Then we which are alive and remain shall be caught up together with them
in the clouds, to meet the Lord in the air:
and so shall we ever be with the Lord.*[11]

In his First Epistle to the Corinthians, the
apostle Paul concludes an elaborate passage on the
resurrection with this further comment on the rapture of those who will still be alive on earth when
Jesus comes:

*Behold, I shew you a mystery; We shall
not all sleep, but we shall all be changed,
In a moment, in the twinkling of an eye,
at the last trump. . .*[12]

These passages, along with a number of
others to the same effect, foretell the bodily resurrection of believers who have "fallen asleep" in
former times, and promise those who remain alive
at Christ's return that they will be suddenly glorified without experiencing physical death.

The final results will be the same in either

case; but oh, how sweet to live in hope, and in the altogether *legitimate* hope, that we may never die!

A New Body

As for the mode of the resurrection, there is invariably someone who asks: "How are the dead raised up? and with what body do they come?"[13]

First, let us consider the *how*.

It is apparent that some "puffed up" fellow in the Corinthian church contrived this question as a rhetorical snare, in an effort to make the most of the implied absurdity of such a hope. It was doubtless his intention to make a "straw man" of the groundless, but not uncommon, contention that the very same particles that composed the natural body will be reassembled to provide the substance of the new one. It is obvious that his purpose was to seize upon a pretext for discrediting the apostle's authentic teaching, while ostensibly "exposing" untenable nonsense based on faulty inferences of his own.

The Scriptures, of course, in no way assert or imply, nor had Paul ever taught, such a ridiculous doctrine.

It is possible that well-intentioned but irresponsible zealots may have fondled such an idea, as alas, some do today, providing scoffers with a plausible excuse to justify their unbelief by pretending to defend the faith against a mischievous superstition.

But not so, Paul. He preached, indeed, that we shall have *new* bodies; but he never intimated that they will be particle-for-particle restorations of our former ones.

Every ordinary school boy knows that the cellular structure of our bodies changes constantly and that in the course of a very few years there is scarcely a single cell, if any, that remains the same as before—unless, perhaps, in our bones.

All of us, by eating food produced on the soil of countless unmarked graves, are constantly assimilating the remains of former generations. This process has been going on for thousands of years. It is preposterous to suppose that millions of people who have shared the same substances, from age to age and generation to generation, can all be clothed with the same original elements each of them surrendered back to mother earth.

All careful Bible students know that, instead of advancing such an insupportable notion, the apostle rebuked the folly of those who were trying to make it a serious issue in the church.

Thou fool, that which thou sowest is not quickened, except it die: And that which thou sowest, thou sowest not that body that shall be, but bare grain, it may chance of wheat, or of some other grain: But God

giveth it a body as it hath pleased him, and
to every seed his own body.[14]

A natural, commonplace occurrence is cited
here to illustrate a supernatural principle, as also
was often done by Jesus in His teaching ministry.
When a grain of wheat or some other grain is
planted, it disintegrates and perishes, so far as its
immediate constitution is concerned. The same
material will never reassume its former arrangement and peculiar properties within a completely
renovated grain. Yet the seed's intrinsic identity,
consisting in its inherent life and nature, survives
the dissolution of its former husk and springs forth
from the scene of death, arrayed in the verdant
splendor of another stalk—essentially the same,
though clothed in newer dress.

"So also is the resurrection of the dead."
Our personal identity will remain unchanged. But
we shall be clothed with bodies which are absolutely new, not simply "made over" from mold and
ashes salvaged from the graves of those who tilled
and nourished on our own. Otherwise, how can
all of them and *all* of us become physically entire
again, since it is evident that all of our natural bodies have shared the same material constituents?

We are to be, at once, the same but glori-
ously different—like the water Jesus turned into
wine at the wedding feast in Cana. At His com-
mand, mere water was taken from the purification

jars and carried to the governor of the feast, who, when he tasted it, called to the bridegroom and exclaimed, "...thou hast kept the good wine until now."[15] As to substantial identity, the "water" and the "wine" were absolutely the same; but as to its condition, the wine was altogether new. And this, I think, is fairly suggestive of the persistence of our individuality in the newness of our heavenly state.

In the case of those who will be "changed"[16] and "caught up"[17] into glory at our Lord's return, the end results of their experience will be the same as if they also had passed through death and been raised up along with the other saints. Although the substance of their bodies will be literally the same as before—transformed, of course—that fact will be merely incidental and of no particular significance in itself.

The purpose of God does not depend upon the meticulous distribution of bodily elements. He has both sufficient wisdom and power to provide new bodies, "as it hath pleased Him," for the living and the dead. What He has done already is ample proof of His ability to perform whatever He is of a mind to undertake. He can impregnate two tiny specks of protoplasm with the vast potentialities of life and humanity. He can fuse them and make a baby that breathes, thinks, talks, loves, hopes, wills, and grows into a Moses, an Aristotle, or a Tennyson. Who would dare consider it incredible that He should fashion new, immortal bodies for those who have already been made to share His moral image and vital breath?

Such is, indeed, the natural thing for an informed believer to expect of such a God! "For our (citizenship) is in heaven; from whence also we look for the Saviour, the Lord Jesus Christ: Who shall change our vile body, that it may be fashioned like unto his glorious body." And if some caviler should insist on asking *how*, it is "according to the working whereby he is able even to subdue all things unto himself."[18]

To Him, "all things are possible;"[19] and those who know Him best are not only confident that He is able to keep His promises but, also, that He "is able to do exceeding abundantly above all that we ask or think."[20]

So much for the *how*; now let us consider the *what*.

Assuming that the dead will rise again, because we have explicit assurance from God to that effect, the question remaining is, "With what bodies do they come?" Only God is fully competent to comprehend this mystery. He has been pleased to give us all the information we need and are able, at the moment, to understand.

Our new body will be characteristically *spiritual*—"It is sown a natural body; it is raised a spiritual body."[21] The present one is "soulical"— the physical organ of natural desires, emotions, and fancies, adapted to the requirements of a material order and subject to the limitations of matter, space, and time. But the new one, though real as the former, will, through a miraculous metamorphosis, be accommodated to conditions on that lofty plane where God and the holy angels inhabit their own congenial element. It will, therefore, be entirely free from the restrictions and barriers to which we are accustomed here, and will be capable of utilizing previously undreamed of resources and opportunities.

It will be *incorruptible*—"It is sown in corruption; it is raised in incorruption."[22] What a prospect! Free from the taint of sin! Immune to the withering sorcery of disease! Invulnerable to the stealthy ambush of declining years! No longer subject to dissipation, deterioration, and decay!

It will be *glorious*—"It is sown in dishonour; it is raised in glory."[23] "This body of our humiliation," as the apostle describes our mortal frame in another passage, descends disgraced by the stigma of sin into an inglorious grave, discarded as an unclean thing. But, like our souls, it, too, has been redeemed. At its resurrection it will radiate the flawless splendor of eternal holiness, never again to become an object of indignity.

It will be *dynamic*—"it is sown in weakness; it is raised in power."[24] On the natural scene, the vigor of youth declines until our mounting infirmities overwhelm us and we find ourselves as helpless as newborn babes. Oh how pathetic it seems when the "evil days come," the "keepers of the house tremble," and the "strong men bow themselves," "the grinders cease because they are few," "those that look out of the windows are darkened," "the grasshopper becomes a burden," "desire fails," and "man goeth to his long home."[25] But, thanks be to God, there is to be another chapter in this story, for those who cherish the "blessed hope." It is a sequel in which our past misfortunes will be reversed and rewarded in "the land where we never grow old"!

It will be an *immortal* body—"For this corruptible must put on incorruption, and this mortal must put on immortality."[26] We shall not only be fitted for glory, immune to sickness, clothed with honor, and endowed with supernatural strength, but shall also be impervious to the stroke of death. Our new estate will be incomparably better than that of Adam before he fell. He was exposed to temptation and the constant liability of sinning, falling, and dying. We, praise God, shall be confirmed in everlasting holiness, health, and immortality!

Like Him!

But there is a capstone that crowns all other promises. In simple words, to which nothing can be added or subtracted, we shall be *like Jesus*. The inspired apostle confidently declares that, "as we have borne the image of the earthy [Adam], we shall also bear the image of the heavenly."[27]

In other words, as surely as we by nature share the character of our racial sire who sinned and fell...by grace, we shall emerge from death in the perfect likeness of our racial Redeemer! Then "our vile body" will be changed, "that it may be fashioned like unto his glorious body."[28] To state the same truth in the inimitable language of the disciple who leaned on Jesus' breast:

> *Beloved, now are we the sons of God, and it doth not yet appear what we shall be: but we know that, when he shall appear, we shall be like him; for we shall see him as he is.*[29]

Our likeness to Christ will not, of course, be restricted to our bodily constitution, though it will certainly involve our glorified physical nature along with other personal qualities. This "likeness" will not consist in identical features and personal peculiarities, but in essential nature and intrinsic character. Else, it would spell the end of any significant individuality, and Christ Himself—not to mention the rest of us—would be a nondescript figure, eternally *incognito,* in a monotonous society of indistinguishable personalities. Since such an absurdity needs no refutation, it will suffice to point out certain recorded facts about our

Lord's post-resurrection appearances. From these facts we may infer what our own condition will be when we become "like Him."

We know from the Scriptures that Jesus, after His resurrection, was able to disengage Himself from His graveclothes without unwinding, or cutting, or tearing away the strips of linen that were coiled around His body from head to foot.[30] What, then, will be "the glorious liberty of the children of God"[31] when we are, likewise, freed from all material encumbrances?

We know that He proceeded forth from a heavily guarded tomb that had been secured with a Roman seal, without so much as waiting for attending angels to remove the entrance stone.[32] Afterward, he entered the "upper room" to greet his assembled disciples while the doors were shut.[33] Do not these marvelous feats suggest that we, when we become "like Him," shall also be able to overcome all temporal obstacles?

We know that He could, at will, conceal or reveal Himself or His identity to natural people. He did this, at first, to Mary,[34] and later to the two disciples He accompanied to Emmaus.[35] He spoke in an audible voice![36] He prepared a meal for His disciples.[37] He even ate with them.[38] But, while He utilized natural things, He was in no way dependent upon them nor limited by natural law.

With no regard to time or space, He could appear wherever He wished, within the compass of a thought[39]—and that, not only on the earth but also in the heavenly domain.[40] In all these things He demonstrated what it will mean to us to be "like Him." If God should offer us our wishes for the asking, could we ask for more?

No doubt there is infinitely more in store for us than we have ever dared to let ourselves expect. There are even incredulous saints who ask, and keep on asking: *Shall we know one another in heaven?*

---

[1] Gen 2:7. [2] I Thess. 5:23. [3] Matt. 27:46; Cf. Ps. 22:1.
[4] Heb. 2:9. [5] Cf. I Cor. 15:55. [6] Cf. Rev. 2:ll; 20:14.
[7] II Cor. 4:14. [8] Luke 24:39. [9] II Cor. 5:1-3.
[10] Cf. Acts 12:15. [11] I Thess. 4:13-17. [12] I Cor. 15:51, 52.
[13] I Cor. 15:35. [14] I Cor. 15:36-38. [15] John 2:10.
[16] I Cor. 15:51; Phil. 3:20, 21. [17] I Thess. 4:17.
[18] Phil. 3:20, 21. [19] Matt. 19:26. [20] Eph. 3:20.
[21] I Cor. 15:44. [22] I Cor. 15:42. [23] I Cor. 15:43.
[24] I Cor. 15:43. [25] Cf. Eccles. 12:1-5. [26] I Cor. 15:53.
[27] I Cor. 15:49. [28] Phil. 3:21. [29] I John 3:2.
[30] Cf. John 20:3-8. [31] Rom. 8:21. [32] Cf. Matt. 28:1-6.
[33] Cf. John 20:19-23. [34] Cf. John 20:14-16.
[35] Cf. Luke 24:13-32; Mark 16:12. [36] Cf. John 21:5.
[37] Cf. John 21:9. [38] Cf. Luke 24:41-43.
[39] Cf. Matt. 28:16, 17. [40] Cf. Luke 24:19; Acts 1:9.

...but then shall I know even as also I am known.

Paul the Apostle

Knowing Each Other In Heaven

This matter is one of the most common concerns, among the bereaved, in modern Christendom. Almost as often as a grave is dug, some anxious person gazes heavenward and wonders, "Will I recognize my loved one when we meet again?"

The answer is found in so many Scriptures that its repetition verges on redundancy: *Of course, we shall know each other over there!*

There is far better reason for asking, *Do we really know each other here?* We can live together—work, sing, pray, and even suffer together—for years on end, and then discover in some unexpected hour of crisis that we never really knew our dearest friends, nor even ourselves! Most of us have had that shocking experience here, but we shall never be startled by such bewildering surprises in "the land of perfect day."

> *For now we see through a glass, darkly; but then face to face: now (we) know in part; but then shall (we) know even as also (we are) known.*[1]

Here, only God can know us as we really are; but, there, we shall know one another as we are known by Him. Nor will it be a matter of simple recognition. We shall enjoy a precious intimacy that will intensify and sweeten our fellowship beyond the fondest expectation of our earthly dreams.

Unmistakable Identity

As a matter of fact, if our personal identity did not provide individual recognition to each of us, it would be virtually meaningless. Even a grain of sand, if closely examined, is distinguishable from any other to be found in all the world. So is every bug, or bird, or blade of grass. The universe teems with individuality, from the atom to the star; yet, individuality means little or nothing unless it is discernible.

This principle finds an even higher expression in the ascending scale from the inanimate to God. He occupies the zenith of individuality— "Hear, O Israel: The LORD our God is one LORD"[2]—which means, of course, among other things, that He transcends and is distinguishable from His handiwork. He has made us like Himself to the extent that each of us subsists as a separate distinctive personal entity. Thus were we born, thus born anew, and thus we shall be resurrected from the dead.

We were foreknown from all eternity,[3] and loved "with an everlasting love,"[4] "chosen" in Christ as special heirs of redeeming grace,[5] and foreordained "to be conformed" to the "image" of our glorified Lord.[6] This means that we, whose "names are written in heaven"[7] and to whom new heavenly names have already been assigned,[8] shall stand as *individuals* before an *Individual* when we render our final account.[9] To be "like Him" will mean to be as recognizable as He is. To deny that we shall know one another in heaven is the same as to say that Christ Himself will neither know us, nor be known by us, in the ages to come.

The entire doctrinal structure of the Bible, including God's redemptive plan and His prophetic program, assumes the persistence of our discernible identities. There are many passages which, apart from such an assumption, could scarcely be either true or meaningful.

For instance, there will be recognition and

differentiation when the righteous dead are raised from among the wicked at our Lord's return. This will happen when Jesus judges "every man" according to his works; when He commands His "sheep" to "sit down with Abraham, Isaac, and Jacob" in the kingdom of God; and when he assigns twelve special thrones to the apostles in the New Jerusalem.

Although we shall undoubtedly be recognized and judged accordingly by God, some might claim that this does not prove we shall know one another. It is sufficient to reply once more with the apostle's categorical assertion:

> *"Then shall* (we) *know even as also* (we are) *known."*[10]

Otherwise, we would not be "at home" in heaven but, instead, would be nameless strangers among our former friends! We would be less well endowed than wicked souls in hell, who, we are told, will recognize the Antichrist when he is damned![11] Else, contrary to the promises, we would not be "like" our glorious Shepherd who knows and calls His sheep by name![12]

The truth is, we shall not only know our former friends and loved ones but shall also find ourselves acquainted with everyone else in the heavenly commonwealth. No introductions were necessary when Peter, James, and John came face to face with Moses and Elijah on "the holy mount." They recognized the heavenly visitants on sight! Likewise, as we have previously observed, the "rich man" in Hades knew and called Abraham by name, though he had never seen him while on earth. If living humans have been known to recognize departed saints, and if a sinner in perdition has been able to identify the soul of a righteous man he never saw before, we shall undoubtedly know more, far more, when we are glorified, than now—not less than mortals on earth and the lost in hell!

So there is every reason for believers to look forward to knowing each other in our future life together. And that plausibly leads to another question: *Will we share alike in heaven?*

---

[1] I Cor. 13:12. [2] Deut. 6:4. [3] Cf. Rom. 8:29.
[4] Jer. 31:3. [5] Cf. Eph. 1:4.
[6] Cf. Rom. 8:29. [7] Luke 10:20.
[8] Cf. Rev. 2:17. [9] Cf. II Cor. 5:10.
[10] I Cor. 13:12. [11] Cf. Isa. 14:9, 10.
[12] Cf. John 10:3, 14.

Rejoice, and be exceeding glad: for great is your reward in heaven...

Matthew the Apostle

Will We Share Alike In Heaven?

"If I can just get to heaven by the skin of my teeth, that will be quite enough and I will be as happy as the rest"—so goes the unwritten confession of many careless Christians who like to surmise that we all shall be blessed exactly alike in the coming world.

Such people reason that, having been saved by grace, we are sure of heaven and, therefore, need not bother much about the way we live in the meantime. We do not, of course, express such thoughts so frankly in our formal creeds. But we publish them, for all the world to read, by what we do and fail to do in our daily lives.

Any of us holding that view is sadly mistaken.

Language lacks sufficient force to duly emphasize the tremendous importance of our present conduct and its inevitable effect upon our fortunes later on. If we are saved at all, it is indeed by grace; but our rewards in glory will be determined altogether by "the things done in (the) body" here and now.[1]

It is true that we shall all be alike in matters pertaining to our "common salvation," as Jude describes it.[2] We shall all have been chosen, redeemed, regenerated, sanctified, and glorified. We shall all be children in the same great Family, fellow members of the selfsame Body, subjects in the same exalted Theocracy. Yet we shall differ, severally, there, precisely as our lives have differed here—as "one star differeth from another star in glory."[3] The apostle Paul wrote to the Corinthians:

> *For we must all appear before the judgment seat of Christ; that everyone may receive the things done in his body... whether it be good or bad.*[4]

The very fact that "every one of us shall give an account of himself to God"[5] implies that our rewards will vary according to our individual merits.

Degrees of Reward

Our salvation, it is true, depends entirely on the merits of the Saviour's redemptive ministry. "For other foundation can no man lay than that is laid, which is Jesus Christ."[6] But it is equally true that, by the grace of God, we determine the extent of our capacity for joy and service in heaven. As we develop our faculties, we thereby lay up within the structure of personal character the precious "building stones" of obedience, on the bedrock of faith. Paul declares:

> *Now if any man build upon this foundation gold, silver, precious stones, wood, hay, stubble; Every man's work shall be made manifest: for the day* [of our accounting, at Christ's return] *shall declare it, because it shall be revealed by fire; and the fire shall try every man's work of what sort it is.*[7]

The Christian can, if he will, use consecration, faithfulness, and similar virtues as moral material—like gold, silver, or marble in an elegant edifice. He can build character that will not only survive the test of discriminative judgment but will also enable him for the realization of heaven's fullest joys and opportunities. Or this same person may foolishly clutter up the inner sanctum of his heart with selfish ambitions, unworthy motives, and immoral rubbish. This collection of wood, hay, or stubble is certain to be consumed by the fire of divine displeasure when we meet the Lord. In either case, the saint himself "goes marching in," by virtue of his redemption through the blood of Christ. But "if any man's work shall be burned, he shall suffer loss [that is, of his rewards]," though "he himself shall be saved; yet so as by fire."[8] This is like a man who escapes with his life from a burning dwelling, while the fruit of all his labor goes up in flames!

It would be impractical in these few pages to attempt an extended discussion of this subject; but let us consider at least a few of the most important principles regarding the apportionment of our future rewards and their effects upon our relative condition in the future world.

Our station in heaven will not be the cause, but the result, of what we *are* within. As we have already observed, the measure of our position and happiness will be limited only by the bounds of our capacities. The boundless riches of heaven will be available to all alike—to "every man according to his eating,"[9] to use a phrase from God's instructions to Israel concerning the paschal feast. We shall all be happy, yes, and fully satisfied; but some with more, and some with less, than our fellow saints.

In a word, the differences in our rewards will correspond to our personal willingness to ap-

propriate, appreciate, and utilize the infinite resources at hand. Just as a seasoned master enjoys
a piece of art much more than a fledgling amateur
possibly can, a saint who has been faithful under
wholesome discipline in the school of Christian
experience will be capable of more delight and
richer achievements than one who has made a habit
of "skipping classes" and "breaking the rules."

Each one of us will have a "full cup," as the
saying goes; but those with larger "cups" will fare
more sumptuously.

However, there will be no rigid *status quo*
in the economy of heaven. According to the Scriptures, we shall all enjoy unending progress and
ceaseless growth. It might be said that our initial
rewards will constitute our capital assets at the
start and that, thenceforth, the constant returns
on our increasing investment will enhance our happiness and usefulness continually, forevermore.

It stands to reason, though, that those who
start ahead at the beginning will enjoy a priceless
advantage throughout the ensuing ages of eternity.

Our Lord often preached on future rewards
and spoke of those who will be "least," and others
who will be "great," when He reviews the record
of our deeds at His return.[10] Several of His leading parables were expressly given to illustrate the
gains and losses of those whose works will be
judged at that time.

As for the apostles, the citations we have

already given from Paul are representative. On this, all Scriptures agree; our right of access to heaven, having been determined by the Father's decree and guaranteed by Christ's redeeming blood, will surely avail for all of us alike, because it is all of grace. On the other hand, our various lots in heaven, being dependent altogether on our works, will correspond, respectively, to the character of our individual earthly careers.

This leads us to consider another question which, though related to the last, requires some further thought: *What will we do in heaven?*

---

[1] II Cor. 5:10. [2] Jude 3. [3] I Cor. 15:41.
[4] II Cor. 5:10. [5] Rom. 14:12.
[6] I Cor. 3:11. [7] I Cor. 3:12, 13.
[8] I Cor. 3:15. [9] Ex. 12:4.
[10] E.g., Matt. 5:12, 19.

What Will We Do Jn Heaven?

According to the Scriptures, there will be rest, sweet rest, but no such thing as idleness, in our heavenly home. We may, instead, look forward to abundant activity, constant progress, unceasing achievement, without a trace of friction, opposition, or disappointment. There will only be the thrill of endless accomplishment hallowed by the Lord's approving smile!

This was by no means true of the ancient saints when they tarried in Sheol-Hades. As "prisoners of hope," they whiled away the passing centuries, waiting—just waiting and hoping. They were comforted, yes; but oh, how they needed comfort while they waited—inactive, unemployed, with nothing to reward their tiresome vigil but the prospect of a better day!

Nor is it altogether true of the saints who are now in the heavenly paradise. They are clothed with the garments of glory. They are "at home" with the Lord. Their condition is better, "far better," than it ever was here; but their felicity is limited, incomplete. If employed at all, and I think they are, they are restricted to purely spiritual activity. They have no bodily facilities with which to undertake new conquests and achieve new triumphs of a tangible sort. They, too, are waiting— happily, but nevertheless, waiting—for a better day.

After the Lord's return, the resurrection of the righteous dead, and the rapture of the living saints, we shall launch forth on a new career of delightful achievement in the tireless, satisfying service of our blessed Lord. It is written that "his servants shall serve him . . . and they shall reign for ever and ever."[1]

Ours will be a royal, priestly service. We shall be engaged as "kings and priests" in the administration of a new Theocracy.[2] As "kings," we shall govern the nations of the millennial earth, each one of us with his own allotted "cities." We shall judge the fallen angels also, ("Do ye not know that the saints shall judge the world? . . . Know ye not that we shall judge angels?")."[3] We shall, as "priests," discharge the pleasant duties of a universal ministry, charged with the conduct of everlasting worship in the heavenly sanctuary.

Surely, this is what the exultant psalmist envisioned when he described our heavenly calling in one of his loveliest beatitudes:

> *Blessed is the man whom thou choosest,*
> *and causest to approach unto thee, that he*
> *may dwell in thy courts: we shall be satis-*
> *fied with the goodness of thy house, even*
> *of thy holy temple.*[4]

There is a shadow, though, that threatens to dull the luster of our hope; for the more we learn about the blessedness that lies in store for us, the more our hearts keep asking: *How can we be happy in heaven, knowing that we have loved ones in hell?*

---

[1] Rev. 22:3, 5.
[2] Cf. Rev. 5:10.
[3] I Cor. 6:2, 3.
[4] Ps. 65:4.

For whosoever shall do the will of God, the same is my brother, and my sister, and mother.

Jesus Christ

Heaven Without Some Loved Ones

Our present meditations would scarcely be complete without a thought or two about this troublesome problem which has caused so many people so much anxiety. The usual tendency is to invent a solution by surmising that we shall never be aware of the fate of those who perish. This is to evade the difficulty by ignoring either known or knowable facts. From what we have already learned, there remains no doubt that both the wicked and the righteous *do* remember their old associates after death and that they *are* aware of one another's lots beyond the grave.

The truth is, that the saints in heaven have no "loved ones" in hell—or none, at least, who are still esteemed as such. They doubtless have many *former* friends and relatives there. But since death terminates all purely temporal relationships, allowing only spiritual bonds to persist, the problem vanishes when it is considered from the heavenly point of view.

In the future state, all men will belong to two entirely different and altogether unrelated families. The children of God will feel no moral sympathy for those of the Enemy. In fact, we shall be so unreservedly devoted to God that we shall actually rejoice when He pronounces judgment on His foes, whoever they are and however closely we may have been associated with them in the natural world.[1]

The question is difficult now because we are accustomed to thinking in terms of cherished earthly ties. After the dissolution of all such purely temporal affinities, we shall find ourselves concerned supremely with the abiding interests of our new estate. Not only that, but we shall perceive and wholeheartedly approve the moral necessity that calls for the exclusion of those who, if admitted, would jeopardize heaven itself by defying the reign of righteousness. Indeed, instead of resenting the sentence of justice against such rebellious unbelievers, we shall heartily extol the "Judge of All the Earth" for rendering it.

The unvarying testimony of the Scriptures to the effect that we shall all be satisfied in heaven, precludes the possibility of grief on account of those who, for no other reason than their own impenitence, are eternally estranged from us by death. If we really love our friends and relatives, now is the time for us to win them, if we can. But if they spurn our concern for them now, their fate will not disturb our eternal bliss with protracted anxiety.

But, I confess, it is with pleasure that I invite your continued attention to a happier theme— *What will our heavenly home be like?*

---

[1] Cf. Rev. 18:20; 19:1, 2.

Eye hath not seen, nor ear
heard, neither have entered into
the heart of man, the things
which God hath prepared for
them that love him.

Paul the Apostle

What Will Our Heavenly Home Be Like?

Desire is a child of character; hope, of desire; and expectation, of hope. It seems that everyone has in the galleries of his own imagination a conception of the kind of "paradise" he wants. One's idea of heaven is both a product and reflection of *what that person is.* Instinctively, we hope for what we cherish most and then, accordingly, we visualize the realization of our own desires.

The American Indian dreamed of a "happy hunting ground." The sensual Mohammedan longs for a celestial harem. The fatalistic Hindu, vexed with perennial frustration, resigns himself to the melancholy prospect of an everlasting coma.

And the carnal Christian fondles the expectation of a grossly material city made of substances as dense and tangible as the gold of Ophir or the adamantine gems on Aaron's breast.

Nobler saints aspire to nobler things—the joyous thrill of communion with God, unclouded fellowship with one another, and the realization of perfect moral and spiritual character. Whatever our several predilections, the Word of God consistently confirms the hope of spiritually-minded people who are more concerned about personal values than physical bonanzas and celestial real estate. Heaven be what it may, to be with Christ and one another in the Father's house will be enough to satisfy our our souls; and whatever else there is besides will be a surplus.

There *will be* such a surplus—a super-abounding plethora of blessedness that will overflow the coffers of desire. Every Biblical description of heaven is apparently meant to heighten the conviction that the land of our inheritance is actually indescribable!

No one can really describe the beauty of a rainbow, the pleasant charm of music, or the flavor of a delicate dessert to someone who has had no previous experiential knowledge of such things. But when addressing those who are familiar with analogous phenomena, we often make use of figures of speech to convey information which is inexpressible in concrete terms. So it is with the inspired descriptions of heaven. They employ analogies and metaphorical allusions to suggest the indescribable grandeur of the glory world to finite creatures who are now unable to think in other than earthly terms.

A Garden

Thus God, in the Holy Scriptures, likens heaven to a beautiful garden, such as that in Eden or the one depicted in the imagery of the Apocalypse.[1] That is, in fact, the meaning of "paradise"— a garden, or park. King Solomon, as well as many other Oriental monarchs, devoted fabulous amounts of money, care, and time to the development of luxurious retreats where he might relax in tranquil peace and comfort. He surrounded himself with every form of beauty Nature and human invention could afford.

But even the loveliest of earthly "paradises" barely serve to typify the surpassing excellence of the one which is reserved for us in "Canaan's fair and happy land"!

A City

The Holy Spirit likens our heavenly home to a beautiful city—a conception which is still, perhaps, more popular than any other among imaginative people almost everywhere.[2] The ancients, too, were especially fond of this symbolical description, the figures of which were so aptly chosen and exquisitely drawn. To nations who gloried in such famous capitals as Babylon, Nineveh, Jerusalem, Athens, and Rome, a great metropolis represented the glory of its founder, the prosperity of its residents, and the safety of its citizens. A beautiful city was a haven of a vast society of kindred folk with common interests, associated together for their mutual welfare and comfort.

But no earthly city could more than faintly foreshadow that "Jerusalem which is above . . . the mother of us all."[3] Her pearly gates bespeak our right of access, as ransomed saints, into the presence of God. Her towering walls, so elegantly garnished with resplendent gems, proclaim the variegate glories of redeeming grace. Her spacious thoroughfare of gold, symbolic of righteous freedom, undergirds the tread of God's elect with imperturbable peace and safety. Her holy river's crystal tide, the fountainhead of life and gladness, flows from the Father's throne to lavish those of "every kindred, and tongue, and people, and nation"[4] with its delights. And her perennial tree, with its healing leaves and life-sustaining fruit, depicts our blessed Saviour as the Personal Embodiment of every good and perfect gift. Truly,

Wondrous things of thee are spoken,
Zion, City of our God!

A Household

The Lord Jesus likens heaven to a "house"—the household of a rich and benevolent Father. He calls it, "my Father's house."[5]

This lovely figure derives its principal significance from patriarchal times, when the head of every family maintained an elaborate establishment for the special benefit of those who were to be his heirs. Of course, he made ample provision for every occupant, servants and all. But he was particularly solicitous for his children, to ensure their personal welfare, safety, and happiness.

Thus Abraham, Isaac, and Jacob must have ordered their households many centuries ago. But the best they could do was like a candle underneath the noonday sun compared to what our Heavenly Father has in store for us. Each of His children will have a mansion; every need will be supplied, and every longing will be gratified.

As the psalmist says,

> *They shall be abundantly satisfied with the fatness of thy house; and thou shalt make them drink of the river of thy pleasures.*[6]

A Home

The great apostle likens heaven to a "home"—a splendid abode adorned with the beauty of love, the ornaments of joy, and the trappings of peace. He reveled in the conviction that "to be absent from the body" is "to be (at home) with the Lord."[7] He deemed it "far better" to die in such a hope than to enjoy a more extended sojourn here.[8]

Delightful prospect! Here on earth there is no sweeter word than "home," nor any privilege more precious than simply being with those we love. We find our greatest satisfaction in the thrill of congenial fellowship and the exhilarating warmth of reciprocal love, around a single hearth and a common table. Yet, the brightest flame of our present bliss is only a flicker in comparison to the surpassing splendor of our heavenly home!

An Inheritance

As a child of God you may safely estimate the riches awaiting you in glory by considering the implications of the longing in your heart. That longing itself is a supernatural gift, for it is obviously unnatural—nay, impossible—for mere creatures of the dust to yearn for the unseen delights of a spiritual realm. Nor do the unregenerate nourish such a hope—they want a harem, a "happy hunting ground," or something else of an equally earthly sort. But we, as Christians, "rejoice in hope of the glory of God"[9]—an aspiration foreign to the natural order, springing from a new, divinely-given heart that craves a spiritual inheritance.

Would God imbue us with such a hope if He did not intend to gratify it? Or does He teach our hearts to yearn for more than He is able to bestow?

Unthinkable!

Yes, of course. But ponder the alternative: if our aspirations *do* reflect the measure of our heritage—at least, until this yardstick proves too short, as it eventually will—this amounts to possessing an "open-sesame" that knows no limits within the realm of moral possibility.

Then, what do we *want?* It will be ours, and "much more" besides! We, according to the Scriptures, are "heirs" of God and "joint-heirs" with Christ, who is "heir of all things."[10] Hence, "all things" are ours and for our sake.[11] If it is true that "no good thing" will be withheld "from them that walk uprightly,"[12] here in the present world, then, what a wealth of glory will be ours when we are made "like Him"! In the prophetic words of the great apostle, "He that spared not his own Son, but delivered him up for us all, how shall he not with him also freely give us all things?"[13]

So, what are we longing for? It will be multiplied to us beyond our power to "ask or think"! If even here and now the lavish blessing often exceeds our utmost expectation and the palms of faith run over with unanticipated joys, oh, what a bounty will be ours when faith, unfettered by sight, extends a confident hand for all that God is able and desirous to impart!

God's Utmost Endowment

Imagine, if you can, what such a God as ours desires to do, knows how to do, and has the power to do for those whom He loved enough to ransom at so dear a cost! Consider Him—the Fountainhead of infinite loving kindness, wisdom, and power—and then ask yourself:

> "What does such love desire for us?
> What does such wisdom plan for us?
> What can such power do for us?"

Unless you can gauge the surge of boundless love, the range of boundless wisdom, and the vast potentialities of boundless power, you must wait for sunrise in glory to manifest what God is contemplating for our personal enrichment in the fragrant bowers of eternity!

Last Christmas season, you doubtless joined the crowds who thronged the streets and malls. Like many, you went from store to store and counter to counter, searching for the most and best your limited funds could purchase for your little ones back home. You knew what they were depending on you to find, buy, and give them for "the big surprise" Christmas morning. Oh, how you tried to make doubly sure that no one would be disappointed when that happy hour arrived! You did your best, your very best—with what you had to spend. But, finding that your means were not as copious as your wishes, you were forced to draw a line far short of your heart's designs. You would have done more, much more, if you could. But human parents have their limitations. We can do so much and, then, however willing, we can do no more.

But such, beloved, is not the case with our Heavenly Father. He is altogether as rich as He is gracious, and as wise and powerful as He is good. He has, from the most remote ages of the past, enlisted all the inexhaustible resources of His omniscience and omnipotence on our behalf, in preparation for the day of our exaltation—"That in the ages to come he might shew the exceeding riches of his grace in his kindness toward us through Christ Jesus."[14] Truly, and no less so now than when these words were first recorded,

> *Eye hath not seen, nor ear heard, neither have entered into the heart of man, the things which God hath prepared for them that love him!*

The Queen of Sheba, in her distant land, heard rumors of Solomon's glory—how his matchless wisdom awed the hearts of envious kings and his mighty achievements had won the admiration of an astonished world. She felt impelled to see and verify these wonders for herself. She made a long and difficult journey to Jerusalem, to visit the king and ascertain the truthfulness of all she had been told. On her arrival, she was graciously received, and Solomon spared no pains to grant her every wish. In his escort she toured his lovely gardens, parks, and pools. She inspected his cedar palace, with its golden trophies, gorgeous furnishings, and ivory throne. She feasted her eyes upon the beautiful temple of the Lord. But her amazement reached its climax, only when, as special guest of honor in the royal court, she witnessed the astounding genius of her host and confessed:

> *O King, when I was at first informed of your remarkable wisdom and accomplishments, I was incredulous, so much so that I dared not trust my ears; but now that I have confirmed all these things for myself, I can only say that the half was never told me of your greatness and the glory of your realm!*[15]

So, I think, it will be with us when our "eyes shall see the king in his beauty"[16] and we behold the land of our inheritance. We, too, are hearing reports, but of One who is "greater than Solomon," reigning in a "better country" than the Queen of Sheba ever dreamed of. Like her, our feeble faith is startled by our ears.

But one bright morning, after we have seen His face, heard His voice, and gazed upon the trophies of His glorious achievements, we shall doubtless fall in joyous ecstasy at His feet. Like the ancient queen, we will confess: "It was a true report, save only that the half was never told!"

For the moment, there remains one final, all-important question which, until we are completely satisfied about its answer, leaves a cloud of doubt between us and our heavenly home. According to the Scriptures, *Who is going to heaven?*

---

[1] Cf. Gen. 2; Rev. 22. [2] Cf. Rev. 21. [3] Gal. 4:26.
[4] Rev. 5:9. [5] John 14:2. [6] Ps. 36:8. [7] II Cor. 5:8.
[8] Cf. Phil. 1:23. [9] Rom. 5:2. [10] Cf. Rom. 8:17; Heb. 1:2.
[11] Cf. I Cor. 3:21; II Cor. 4:15. [12] Ps. 84:11. [13] Rom. 8:32.
[14] Eph. 2:7. [15] Cf. II Chron. 9. [16] Isa. 33:17.

And this is the will of him that sent me, that every one which seeth the Son, and believeth on him, may have everlasting life...

John the Apostle

Who Is Going To Heaven?

Everything we have learned thus far, however wonderful, will go for naught so far as you are concerned, unless by placing your trust in Jesus you become a citizen of the heavenly commonwealth. There is nothing wanting in God's provision for our future. But what about our eligibility for receiving it? Are we prepared, as children of God, to share in the inheritance? Have we made our "calling and election" sure?

Beloved, we cannot afford to remain in doubt about this matter. For doubt itself is an indication that saving faith is either lacking altogether or that, otherwise, the apprehensive believer is woefully ill-informed. While the Scriptures nowhere teach that all of those who lack assurance are unsaved, the fact remains that those who are still uncertain *may* be lost. And that is a needless risk for anyone to take, since any real believer may confirm his hope of glory by acquainting himself with the elementary teaching of the Word of God.

Have you done that? If not, by all means do so; but beware of religious delusions, for false assurance is fraught with far more peril than no assurance at all.

A person may be as religious as Cain, and yet be rejected of God:[1]

¤ He may be a descendant of Abraham, and still become a reprobate—like Ahab, for instance, who "sold (him)self to work evil in the sight of the LORD"[2]

¤ He may be a veritable paragon of outward morality, but fail to enter the kingdom—like the "rich young ruler," who took great pride in keeping the letter of the Law but "went away sorrowful" when he might have received the gift of eternal life.[3]

¤ He may be a nominal Christian without possessing a real experience of grace—like Simon Magus who, despite his formal profession, had no "part nor lot" with the regenerate brotherhood.[4]

¤ He may, like Judas, be a preacher[5] or, like the seven sons of Sceva,[6] cast out demons, and be himself a "son of perdition," having "no home, and without God in the world."

It is not enough to pay lip service to Jesus and perform religious chores, for He Himself warns:

> *Not every one that saith unto me, Lord, Lord, shall enter the kingdom of heaven; but he that doeth the will of my Father which is in heaven. Many will say to me in that day, Lord, Lord, have we not prophesied in thy name? and in thy name have cast out devils? and in thy name done many wonderful works? And then will I profess unto them, I never knew you: depart from me, ye that work iniquity.*[7]

Here, Jesus makes it clear that only those who do the Father's will are really saved. And "this," He tells us elsewhere, "is the will of him that sent me, that every one which seeth the Son, and believeth on him, may have everlasting life."[8]

It *is not* God's will for us, poor sinners that we are, to pretend that we are personally religious. God's will *is* for us to be saved by trusting the One He sent to lavish us with mercy in spite of our ill-deserts. We are not saved by proving our worthiness, nor by trying to make amends for our

121

misdeeds. We find assurance only by trusting the Lord Jesus Christ for "all things that pertain unto life and godliness."⁹

We can profess religion, join the church, observe the "sacraments," and devote ourselves to the abstemious life of a modern Pharisee. But we shall never be sure of heaven until we rest our souls entirely on the finished work of Christ, instead of trying to justify ourselves by what we say or do. Religious unbelievers who lull their consciences with false assurance do so only by ignoring their own demerits and underestimating the righteous standard by which they must be judged. As for those of us who have been brought to see the terrible distance between what we are and what God's righteousness requires of us, we know ourselves too well to hope at all—*until we learn to anchor our hope in Christ alone!*

Then, doubting ceases and our hearts are girded with sober confidence. Once we are convinced that we have been redeemed "from all iniquity," we know that we have been "justified by his grace" that "we should be made heirs according to the hope of eternal life."¹⁰

From then on, there remains no judgment for us to fear. We are assured that, having been once and for all acquitted at the bar of divine justice, we shall never again find ourselves exposed to jeopardy. Such is the testimony of the Saviour Himself. He declares, as it were, with a solemn oath: "Verily, verily, I say unto you, He that heareth my word, and believeth on him that sent me, hath [present tense] everlasting life, and shall not come into condemnation [or, literally, *judgment*]; but is passed from death unto life."[11] It is this profound assurance that enables us to grasp the full significance of His farewell promise:

> *Let not your heart be troubled: ye believe in God, believe also in me. In my Father's house are many mansions: if it were not so, I would have told you. I go to prepare a place for you. And if I go and prepare a place for you, I will come again, and receive you unto myself; that where I am, there ye may be also.*[12]

If you have not yet found this blessed assurance, your difficulty has to do with your *relationship with Christ*, not something else. It is either that no saving relationship has been established, or that you have failed to inform yourself on what the Scriptures teach about your spiritual experience. It goes without saying that a person who is still unsaved cannot make sure of heaven unless he first makes peace with God. But it is possible, and indeed a very common thing, for uninstructed or misinstructed believers to be so utterly confused that they are never really sure of anything.

For instance, when, contrary to the Scriptures, we persist in looking at ourselves instead of looking to Christ alone, it is inevitable that we must feel condemned and suffer needless doubts.

Does Satan sometimes wake you up at midnight, shouting: "You're a sinner! You're a sinner! Only saints are saved!"?

Then, just admit it. Hurl your Bible in his face and re-apprise him, and mainly yourself, of the fact that "Christ Jesus came into the world to save *sinners.*"[13]

Does he attempt to undermine your confidence, by retorting: "How could Jesus save a stupid, worthless blunderer like you?"

Then, just confess that, according to the Law, you deserve to die;[14] and then take refuge in the fact that Jesus died your death that you might live.[15]

Of course, we are sinners—helpless and deserving only the wrath of God. But "Christ died for our sins."[16] "He was wounded for our transgressions, he was bruised for our iniquities: the chastisement of our peace was upon him; and with his stripes we are healed."[17] He "suffered for sins, the just for the unjust, that he might bring us to God."[18] Therefore, "He that believeth on him is not condemned!"[19]

If the Tempter replies (as some of his ministers do) that you have sinned *since* being saved and, therefore, these "exceeding great and precious promises" no longer avail for you, do not be dismayed. Admit the truth and answer his perverted logic with the Word of Truth.

Of course, you have sinned since you were saved. Even James confesses that "in many things" we all stumble.[20] But God has, nevertheless, made ample provision for our correction, forgiveness, and continued safety.

> *If we confess our sins, he is faithful and just to forgive us our sins, and to cleanse us from all unrighteousness.*[21]

If we attempt to persist in disobedience, He chastens us "for our profit, that we might be partakers of his holiness."[22] "If we are (faithless), he abideth faithful; for he cannot deny himself."[23] And to cover all such cases, we are given these emphatic words from the mouth of our Lord Himself:

> *My sheep hear my voice, and I know them, and they* [as to their normal course of conduct] *follow me: And I give unto them eternal life; and they shall never perish* [get lost, or destroy themselves—Greek middle voice], *neither shall any* (one) *pluck them out of my hand. My Father, which gave them me, is greater than all; and no* (one) *is*

able to pluck them out of my Father's hand.[24]

The Lord Jesus Christ Himself is our Salvation. He is the Ground of our assurance, and the Guarantor of our security. Therefore, it is written that, "Whosoever believeth on him shall not be ashamed."[25] *This means that those who are reposing their trust in Him will never be disappointed in the world to come!* Nor even now, so far as our peace of mind depends on Him. We are often disappointed in ourselves, but never in Him—so great is His faithfulness!

Still, as gladly as we flee from self to God for refuge in every storm, we sometimes find it surprisingly hard to interpret the fortunes of our fellow men accordingly. It is somehow easier to hope that God will be exceedingly gracious to us, than to believe that He is equally merciful to others who share our own infirmities. As a consequence, many of us suffer a good deal of needless anxiety for our departed loved ones who have faltered along the way. In my opinion, we might find it helpful in this connection to reread the Psalms occasionally—especially those with lines like these:

> *If thou, LORD, shouldest mark iniquities, O Lord, who shall stand? But there is forgiveness with thee, that thou mayest be feared.*[26]

or these:

> *He hath not dealt with us after our sins;*
> *nor rewarded us according to our*
> *iniquities...For he knoweth our frame; he*
> *remembereth that we are dust.*[27]

Some of us are slow to remember that our dying friends are still encumbered with the frailties of sinful flesh and that the old rebellious nature continues its embarrassing activity until the final breath. We are also prone to overlook the fact that all the frustrated forces of nature combine to harass a person during his declining years and ebbing hours.

When I was a boy, I treasured among my special friends an elderly man who was considered one of the most saintly Christians in our community. No one would have thought of questioning his integrity—until he fell ill with pellagra and, while delirious, used some rather obstreperous language he had evidently heard, and possibly acquired by practice before he was saved. I myself could not, in those early days, account for his deplorable lapse. But even then, I did not agree with some of his neighbors who lifted their eyebrows and muttered, "The old man's fallen from grace!"

Since then, I have learned that it was not a spiritual "lapse" at all. It was not my dear old friend who was saying those ugly words, but his carnal nature taking advantage of its final opportunity to express itself. The same thing often happens when a person is under anesthesia—ask the doctors and nurses! It may happen to you. It may have happened already to someone you love. In your case, you are quick to make all possible allowances for extenuating circumstances. Why not make the same allowances for others?

A person's fate does not depend on how his old Adamic nature reacts to the infirmities of age or the throes of death, but on whether or not he has been truly born anew by trusting the Lord Jesus Christ. If he has, the "new man" will be shouting in glory when the "old man" lies forever silenced in the grave!

I used to wonder why God recorded the drunkenness of Noah, the debauchery of Samson, the adultery of David, the doubting of Thomas, the denials of Peter, and similar sins of other ancient saints, for all the world to read. That was before I had learned the truth about human depravity and the Gospel of the Grace of God. I am now convinced that He included all those "lapses" in the record, first, to warn us against such follies but, also, to assure us that a God who could save and keep such people as they, can be depended upon to save and keep us too! He chastened them for their remissness and will chasten us for ours; but as surely as they are in heaven—*and they are*[28]— we, too, are going there!

128

So, we must not allow some legalistic Pharisee to torture our minds by pointing out the frailties of our loved ones who are gone. We should deplore their faults and resolve to avoid them, and every true Christian will join us in such noble sentiments; but if our departed friends were really trusting the Lord Jesus Christ, it is not they, but the critical Pharisee, who needs our concern. An erring saint will lose some of his reward in heaven, "but he himself shall be saved."[29] A Pharisee "has his reward"[30] right here on earth – the admiration of men – but he will lose his soul when he has paid his final tithe and prayed his final prayer![31]

Some years ago there was a fine young Christian man in the mountains of North Carolina who fell among wicked companions and eventually disgraced himself. Shortly afterward, a godly old country doctor was called to the prodigal's bedside. He immediately recognized the signs of approaching death.

"My boy," he said, "I feel that I owe it to you to tell you the truth; you are about to die and, in my opinion, it will not be very long. Are you ready to meet the Lord?"

The dying youth, who knew all too well that he had erred but also knew that he was trusting the Lord, replied;

"Christ died for *sinners*, Doctor Jones; and *I* am *one!*"

A religious unbeliever may see nothing but

tragedy in such an experience, but a Bible-believing Christian sees a rainbow in the threatening cloud. It is, to be sure, a dreadful warning against the fearful cost of disobedience. It is also a reminder that, even in death, a wayward saint has more and better ground for hope than any Pharisee!

Oh how much better to receive an "abundant entrance" into the heavenly kingdom than to be "saved; yet so as by fire!"[32] Such is the privilege of those who crown their faith with lives of faithfulness—like a saintly old "mother in Israel" who, back in my little home town long years ago, crossed over Jordan in a blaze of glory, shouting the victory. When the hour of her departure came she turned to my mother and, with the radiance of heaven beaming from her face, exclaimed: "Sister Heatherley, for a long, long time, I have looked forward to this moment. For many years I feared it, dreading to see it come; but now that it is here, I want you to know that my passing is brighter than noonday!"

As for you and me, I hope it may please our gracious Lord to let us live until He comes. How wonderful, should we be caught up suddenly, without a moment's separation from our loved ones or the anguish of telling anyone goodbye, to be with Him and one another in our Father's house! But if that be denied, the Lord knows best.

If it be His will for us to take our journey

through "the valley of the shadow of death," then we may "fear no evil," for he will be with us, his "goodness and mercy" will follow us, and we shall "dwell in the house of the Lord for ever."

---

[1] Cf. Gen. 4:5. [2] I Kings 21:20. [3] Cf. Luke 18:23.
[4] Acts 8:21. [5] Cf. Matt. 10:1-8. [6] Cf. Acts 19:13-16.
[7] Matt. 7:21-23. [8] John 6:40. [9] II Pet. 1:3.
[10] Titus 2:14; 3:7. [11] John 5:24. [12] John 14:1-3.
[13] I Tim. 1:15. [14] Cf. Ezek. 18:4. [15] Cf. Gal. 2:20.
[16] I Cor. 15:3. [17] Isa. 53:5. [18] I Pet. 3:18.
[19] John 3:18. [20] James 3:2, ASV. [21] I John 1:9.
[22] Cf. Heb. 12:5-11. [23] II Tim. 2:13. ASV. [24] John 10:27-29
[25] Rom. 10:11. [26] Ps. 130:3, 4. [27] Ps. 103:10, 14.
[28] Cf. Heb. 11. [29] I Cor. 3:15. [30] Matt. 6:5.
[31] Cf. Matt. 23. [32] Cf. II Pet. 1:11; I Cor. 3:15.

O death, where is thy sting?
O grave, where is thy victory?

Paul the Apostle

Appendix

Further Thoughts on Our Lord's Post-Crucifixion Ministry in Sheol-Hades

A continuation of the discussion on pages 47-58.

I am aware, of course, that there are of late some fairly respectable writers who flatly deny that Jesus descended into Hades after His death. Their ineffectual efforts to refute this doctrine have not resulted from any valid scholarly objections but, rather, from their fear of its possible implications in other areas of Biblical interpretation:

¤ For instance, those who believe in Purgatory and Universal Reconciliationists use it as a buttress for their misinterpretation of I Peter

3:18-20. They hold that confirmed unbelievers in Hades will be granted another, more availing, opportunity to be saved. It is inadmissible, however, to repudiate a self-evident truth in an attempt to support a position that cannot be substantiated by other evidence.

¤ The opponents of the well-nigh universally accepted doctrine that Jesus descended into Hades, rely almost entirely on a single argument —the fact that the original text of Acts 2:27 may be rendered, "Thou wilt not *abandon* My soul *unto* Hades," instead of, "Thou wilt not *leave* my soul *in* hell (Hades)." The difference depends principally on the variable meaning of a three-letter preposition. They contend that their preferred translation indicates that Jesus' soul did not go to Hades after the manner of other disembodied human spirits in pre-Crucifixion times.

I have no objection to their favorite rendering itself; but, for several cogent reasons, I am compelled to reject the inference they extort from it. The peculiar wording they insist upon is neither necessitated nor invalidated by appealing to the sense the same Greek verb exhibits in other New Testament passages.[1] It is obvious that this verb is capable of various usages, depending on the context in which it happens to occur. So far as I know, no one denies that the Greek original permits the substitution of "abandon . . . unto" in the place of "leave . . . in".[2] But the basic meaning is virtually the same in either case.

Dr. W. O. Carver recognizes this point in his commentary on the Book of Acts. For, while he gives the translation, "Thou wilt not *leave* My soul *unto* Hades," he explains that, "David was speaking for God and in confidence looked forward to One, the fruit of his loins, the Christ whose soul *could not remain* in the place of spirits that are separated from their bodies while their bodies decay."[3]

No one who is familiar with the Apostles' Creed and its *"He descended into hell (Hades)"* clause, can doubt that this has been the prevailing view of Christians in general from time immemorial. Moreover, most of the leading theologians of Christendom have vigorously defended this tenet against all attacks.

Dean Plumptre, a Biblical exegete of no mean stature, remarks: "It is suggestive, at all events, to note the wide *consensus* of men of different schools of thought in favor of the interpretation: all, or nearly all, the Fathers who notice the passage at all, all the great Roman Catholic, Lutheran and Anglican commentators, modern scholars as widely separated from each other as Meyer, Delitzch, Ewald among the Germans; Ellicott, Wordsworth, and Alford among ourselves."[4]

Dr. Kenneth Wuest, among recent authorities on the Greek New Testament, writes: "In Acts 2:27, 31, our Lord at His death went to Hades, the passage in Acts being quoted from Ps. 16:10, where the Hebrew is 'Sheol.' His soul was not *left in* Hades, the 'paradise' portion, nor did His body in Joseph's tomb see corruption, for He was raised from the dead on the third day. He as the Man Christ Jesus, possessing a human soul and spirit, as He possessed a human body, entered the abode of the righteous dead, having committed the keeping of His spirit to God the Father (Luke 23:46)."[5]

It is nothing short of preposterous for one to allow his personal bias to seize upon a questionable inference from a variable preposition in an isolated text, in an effort to destroy the keystone of a doctrine the ramifications of which are clearly discernible throughout the Bible. The stake is too great to be taken lightly, and it is far more vital than some good people seem to realize. For our Lord's post-Crucifixion ministry in Sheol-Hades is indissociably connected with His redemptive mission on behalf of God's elect in both the old and new dispensations. To the former, it meant immediate release from detention; and, in its effect, it prevents our being detained at all.

Because of our involvement in Adam's guilt, we were *all* consigned to Sheol. Prior to Jesus' death and resurrection, it was normal for all men to be confined, at death, within the 'lower parts of the earth'—the wicked[6] and the righteous,[7] alike. We know from Jesus' teaching in Luke 16:19-31, that there was an intervening "gulf" between the tormented sinners and the comforted saints in that "unseen realm;" but deceased believers could not escape their prison and enter heaven until after they had been redeemed. And since it was *men* who had sinned, deliverance had to be wrought by a *Man* who was "in all points" like the rest of us, "apart from sin"—a Saviour who would have a human birth, live a human life, die a human death, and as a human Conqueror join His people in Sheol in order to lead them forth, according to the promises.

Such was precisely what the prophets had told believers of the pre-Christian era to expect— a hope bound up in the personal ministry of the Lord Jesus Christ. The cheerful prophecy, "Thou wilt not leave my soul in Sheol," not only vouchsafed the Saviour's personal deliverance from the underworld, but also envisioned the liberation of those for whom He died.

It was this assurance that emboldened the ancient Israelite to sing, "But God will redeem my soul from the power of the grave;"[8] and it likewise prompted David to construe his own triumphal procession to the sanctuary as a type of the risen Christ escorting the liberated saints into the heavenly paradise, as expressed in his exultant words: "Thou hast ascended on high, thou hast led captivity captive: thou hast received gifts for men; yea, for the rebellious also, that the LORD God might dwell among them."⁹

Moreover, God confirmed this hope with explicit promises, from time to time. Through the prophet Hosea, He declared: "I will ransom them [the elect] from the power of Sheol; I will redeem them from death: O death, where are thy plagues? O Sheol, where is thy destruction?"¹⁰ And he spoke proleptically through Zechariah to the same effect:

> As for thee also [that is, Christ], by the blood of thy covenant I have sent forth thy prisoners [deceased old dispensation saints] out of the pit wherein is no water; and then, addressing the imprisoned saints themselves, He continued: Turn you to the strong hold [the heavenly 'Zion'], ye prisoners of hope: even to day do I declare that I will render double unto thee.¹¹

Against this backdrop, Jesus used the typical experience of Jonah to illustrate His imminent descent into Sheol-Hades: "For," He declared, "as Jonas was three days and three nights in the whale's belly; so shall the Son of man be three days and three nights in the heart of the earth"¹²— language which, though it doubtless implies the burial and resurrection of Jesus' body, actually asserts that He Himself would spend three days and nights, not in a peripheral terrestrial tomb, but in the central depths of the earth.

The Saviour's later promise concerning the Church, that "the gates of hell (Hades)" should not "prevail against it,"[13] may be understood readily enough in the light of the foregoing facts. Instead of merely guaranteeing the perpetuity of the visible historical Church, as we are sometimes told, He was assuring His disciples that His sacrifice for sin would make it impossible for Sheol-Hades any longer to restrain its "prisoners of hope" or to detain the rest of us at all!

Our Lord's description of conditions in Hades prior to His crucifixion, as recorded in the 16th chapter of Luke, accords with all that we have learned thus far and affords us much additional light on subsequent events. His promise to the dying thief, "To day shalt thou be with me in paradise,"[14] alludes, accordingly, to "Abraham's bosom," or the region in Sheol-Hades which was occupied by God's elect; though "paradise," according to Paul, has been in heaven since the purging of the heavenly sanctuary by the risen Saviour.[15]

Since, in their ceaseless evangelistic efforts, all the apostles were occupied almost exclusively with the major emphases of the Gospel, none of them took the trouble to compose an elaborate treatise on this special theme. But in their presentation of the more immediate aspects of the Christian message, they occasionally made allusions which are coherent only on the supposition that they knew and believed these things.

Peter's citation from the 16th Psalm, as recorded in Acts 2:27, 31, presents such a case. For it could scarcely have been an accident that the very man who was so recently assured by Jesus that "the gates of hell (Hades)" should not prevail against the Church, was now assuring the Militant Church that Jesus' soul had not been left in Hades, but that He had fulfilled God's purpose in redeeming the Mystical Church and emerging from the clutches of death as its glorified Head—"both Lord and Christ."

It is likewise unbelievable that Peter, had he not been convinced of Jesus' descent into Hades, would have injected the following statement into his First Epistle:

> *Christ also suffered for sins once, the righteous for the unrighteous, that he might bring us to God; being put to death in the flesh, but made alive in the spirit; in which also he went and preached unto the spirits in prison, that aforetime were disobedient, when the longsuffering of God waited in the days of Noah . . .*[16]

Here the apostle is in the midst of an exhortation to faithfulness during persecution, and is pointing to the triumph Jesus wrought through suffering, as an example for the instruction and encouragement of the Saviour's followers. He is about to tell us that the imagery of Christian baptism which depicts the Saviour's death and resurrection, is also meant to picture our own experience; but instead of making a bald assertion to that effect, he illustrates the meaning of baptism with a familiar Old Testament type—the patriarch Noah's deliverance from the Flood by means of the very waters that threatened his life. In the transition of his thoughts from Christ to Noah, Peter is reminded of a subsequent encounter between Jesus and those who had perished in the Flood; and, in a casual but very definite way, he tells us that, though those now-disembodied antediluvians "aforetime [prior to the event now under consideration] were disobedient," nevertheless, Jesus "went and preached unto (their) spirits in prison."

He does not say that the Holy Spirit or the spirit of the pre-incarnate Son of God preached through the mouth of Noah to fleshly people who, while still alive on earth, were disobedient, but that the quickened human spirit of the disembodied Christ "went and preached" to "the spirits" who were "in prison," having "aforetime" been disobedient "when the longsuffering of God waited in the days of Noah." It is an undebatable fact that the *human* spirit of the Man Jesus Christ had no existence, as such, in Noah's day, not to mention the further fact that He had not as yet been "quickened" at that time.

But it would be a waste of time to answer the evasive theories which have been devised in an attempt to circumvent the obvious teaching of this passage. It means precisely what it says. Although, as to His physical nature, our Lord had been put to death, His personal spirit was quickened to fit Him for His new and glorious career in the spiritual realm. And He, in His quickened human spirit, "went and preached unto the spirits in prison, that *aforetime* were disobedient"— that is, to the disembodied anti-diluvians in Hades.

Without examining this particular passage any further at the moment, we may find a good deal of additional confirmation for our previous conclusions, and also some new details of utmost significance, by considering the implications of a related verse in the very next chapter. Without any break whatever in his general line of argument, Peter goes on to say, "for this cause was the gospel preached also to them that are dead, that they might be judged according to men in the flesh, but live according to God in the spirit."[17]

This verse looks back to the preceding one, in which we are told that Christ is "ready to judge the quick [the living] and the dead." It recalls the previous reference to Jesus' having preached to "the spirits in prison," in order to explain why disembodied sinners can be justly judged along with the living. The Gospel was preached "*also* [or, *even*] to them," in order that they might be judged after the same manner as those who had heard it while in the flesh, to the end that, should they be disposed to accept it, they might, in keeping with God's gracious purposes, live after the manner of His own exalted life in the spiritual sphere.

This does not mean that any who have heard and rejected the Gospel in this life will accept it and be saved after death. If it did, it would flatly contradict a number of other passages which plainly teach the very opposite.[18] It does, however, show that ample provision is made for those who have never heard nor rejected the Gospel here, thus justifying God in passing sentence against them if, on hearing it, they reject it later on.

This, while leaving a good many questions still unanswered, goes a long way toward relieving the problem as to how unnumbered millions of people who have never yet heard the Gospel, can and will be held accountable in the day of judgment. They will have to hear it before they can be condemned for rejecting it,[19] or before they can be born again.

According to the consistent teaching of the Scriptures, we are bound to assume that all of God's elect among them will eventually hear and accept it. The same is true of irresponsible children who die before attaining to an age of moral responsibility. Although their racial guilt has been expiated by Christ, they, like the rest of us, must hear and accept the Gospel in order to be justified and born again. Both justification and regeneration are wrought through faith;[20] "faith cometh by hearing, and hearing by the word of God;"[21] and we can be "begotten" only "with the word of truth."[22]

This conclusion, although based on familiar truths which are regarded as axiomatic among all thoroughgoing Evangelicals, may jar the ears of some who have another, less logical, way of pronouncing "shibboleth;" but since it necessitates no suppositions contrary to anything that has been revealed, it presents no insurmountable difficulties to reverent faith.

It is not explicitly asserted that such preaching is being done in the unseen world today, nor are we told just how or by whom it might be done. But we are bound to assume the fact from the precedent, and every Bible student knows that there are numerous ways by which it may be done. It is a matter of common knowledge that Jesus Himself set the precedent; that God is "no respecter of persons;" that there are still vast numbers of people who die without ever having heard, or accepted, or rejected the Gospel; and that the moral necessities and divine provisions for such a ministry are as real and relevant now as they have ever been. Moreover, however little we may know about related details, the *fact* itself stands in the sacred record along with all the other tenets of "the most holy faith."

The apostle Paul, like Peter, made several significant allusions to our Lord's post-Crucifixion ministry in Hades, implicitly confessing it as an authentic Christian doctrine, without expounding it at length. For instance, in Romans 10:7, there is this question: "Who shall descend into the deep [or, literally, *the abyss*]? (that is, to bring up Christ again from the dead)," he makes faith reply that "God hath raised him from the dead"— an argument which definitely and necessarily implies that Christ was in the "deep" (or, *abyss*) just prior to His resurrection.

Again, in I Corinthians 15:55, ("O death, where is thy sting? O grave [or, literally, *Hades*], where is thy victory?"), he exults in the fulfillment of Hosea's prophecy[23] to the effect that Christ would liberate the old dispensation saints from Sheol-Hades, securing for both them and us eternal victory over its restraining power.

But his most explicit reference to this general line of truth is found in Ephesians 4:8-10, as follows: "Wherefore he [the Holy Spirit, when He indited the words about to be quoted from Psalm 68:18] saith, 'When he [Christ] ascended up on high, he led captivity captive, and gave gifts unto men.' [The quote ends, and Paul injects the following parenthetical remarks, before resuming his main line of thought:] (Now that he ascended, what is it but that he also descended first into the lower parts of the earth?[24] He that descended is the same also that ascended up far above all heavens, that he might fill [or, *fulfill*] all things.)"

Having exhorted us to prosecute our several callings in a manner conducive to the realization of the ideal unity we have in Christ, the apostle is about to explain that, though we share alike in all vital essentials, we are very differently endowed with spiritual gifts. That is his principal theme, but he digresses for a moment to explain the historical origin of our special gifts. They were conferred upon the Church by the risen Saviour after He had "descended first into the lower parts of the earth" and "led captivity captive," to fulfill the types of Psalm 68:18, where David tells us how he led the hosts of Israel to the newly-constructed sanctuary of the Lord. In other words, Paul believed that Jesus, after His death, descended into Sheol-Hades, delivered the old dispensation saints, and led them into the heavenly sanctuary, before conferring the gifts of the Holy Spirit on the Church's earthly complement at Pentecost.

Nor were Peter and Paul the only apostles who clung to this belief; for, at the very close of the Apostolic age, we find the disciple who "leaned on Jesus' breast" making mention of those who are "under the earth," foretelling the day when "death and hell (Hades)" will be "cast into the lake of fire," and reminding us that Jesus has the "keys of hell (Hades)"![25]

Truly,

> *The secret things belong unto the LORD our God: but those things which are revealed belong unto us and to our children for ever. . .* [26]

---

[1] Cf. Matt. 27:46; Mark 15:34; Rom. 9:28; II Cor. 4:9; II Tim. 4:10, 16; Heb. 10:25; 13:5 – in all of which passages the Authorized Version renders the word in question with some form of the verb "forsake," except in Acts 2:27, 31, and Rom. 9:28, where it is rendered with various tenses of "leave."

[2] This, with slight variations, is substantially the rendering given by the A.S.V., R.S.V., C. B. Williams, Rotherham, The Twentieth Century N.T., and several critical commentaries; but the sense of the Authorized Version is retained by Moffatt, Goodspeed, Weymouth, Montgomery, Darby, The 1911 Bible, Douay, and Vincent.

[3] *The Acts of the Apostles* (Broadman), pp. 30, 31. My italics.

[4] *The Spirits in Prison* (Isbister, London, 1893), p. 109.

[5] *Treasures in the Greek N.T.* (Eerdmans), p. 46. My italics.

[6] Cf. Ps. 63:9; Ezek. 26:20; 31:14, 16, 18; 32:18, 24; and, in particular: Num. 16:30; Job 21:7, 13; Prov. 9:18; Isa. 14:15; Matt. 12:23; Luke 16:23.

---

[7] Cf. Ps. 139: 15, 16; Isa. 44:23; and, in particular:
Gen. 37:35; Job 14:13; Ps. 16:10; 89:48; Luke 16:22.

[8] Ps. 49:15. [9] Ps. 68:18. [10] Hosea 13:14, A.S.V.

[11] Zech. 9:11, 12. [12] Matt. 12:40.

[13] Matt. 16:18. [14] Luke 23:43.

[15] Cf. II Cor. 12:1-4; Heb. 9:22-24; 10:19 f.

[16] I Pet. 3:18-20, A.S.V. [17] I Pet. 4:6.

[18] E.g., Matt. 12:31, 32 and John 3:18, 36, both of which passages assert the same thing; or, namely, that those who, having heard the truth, deliberately reject it, are irrecoverably lost. Such is the meaning of "believeth not" in John 3:18, 36 – "a permanent attitude or refusal" (A. T. Robertson, *Word Pictures in the N.T.*, in loco).

[19] Jesus tells us that "he that believeth not is condemned already, *because he hath not believed in the name of the only begotten Son of God*," adding, "and this is the condemnation, that light is come into the world, and men loved darkness rather than light" (John 3:18, 19). Since it is rejecting the Son of God, or refusing the light of the Gospel, that condemns, no one can be finally condemned unless and until he hears and rejects God's testimony concerning His Son.

[20] Cf. Rom. 3:28; John 1:12; Acts 16:31; Eph. 2:8, 9;
I John 5:1.

[21] Rom. 10:17. [22] James 1:18; cf. I Pet. 1:23.

[23] Hosea 13:14. [24] Cf. Ps. 139:15; 16:10; Matt. 12:40; Acts 2:27, 31; Rom. 10:7; I Pet. 3:18-20; 4-6.

[25] Rev. 5:3; 20:14; 1:18. [26] Deut. 29:29.

About the Author

E. X. Heatherley's last change of residence came on June 8, 1997, when he joined friends, parishioners, and loved ones in the place described so eloquently in *Our Heavenly Home*. He was eighty-eight.

His journey on this planet encompassed more than sixty years as a Christian minister, pastoring ten churches, four of which he founded. As a youth, he attended Wake Forest College, and like many ministers in those days, he entered the pastorate without a formal seminary education. However, being gifted with rare communications skills, brilliant intellect, and a relentless impetus to learn and pass on the truths of the Christian Scriptures, Heatherley spent the better part of the twentieth century studying the Bible, the biblical languages, and the writings of Christian scholars and leaders from biblical times to the present.

The joy of his life was passing on the truths he discovered to as many Christians and potential Christians as he possibly could. He did this through preaching and teaching in his pastorates, Bible classes and evangelistic meetings in scores of other churches, Bible and Greek classes for young ministers, his radio ministry (introduced on the air as "The Man With The Book"), and writing, publishing and distributing unnumbered books, pamphlets, and a magazine called "Grace and Glory."

Heatherley's last manuscript, a comprehensive study of the parables of Christ (*The Parables of Christ*, Balcony Publishing) was released a few days before his death.

He and his wife, Hettie Lee (Langston) were married for sixty-six years. They spent most of their life and ministry in North Carolina and Florida. Hettie joined Erskine in their *heavenly home* six months after his passing. Their family includes six children and twenty-five grandchildren.

—*The Editors*

For more information about works by E. X. Heatherley, call 1-800-777-7949.